Evolution and Culture

Evolution and Culture

EDITED BY **MARSHALL D. SAHLINS & ELMAN R. SERVICE**
FOREWORD BY **LESLIE A. WHITE**

by Thomas G. Harding
David Kaplan
Marshall D. Sahlins
Elman R. Service

THE UNIVERSITY OF MICHIGAN PRESS

ANN ARBOR PAPERBACKS

First edition as an Ann Arbor Paperback 1988
First paperback edition 1982
Copyright © by the University of Michigan 1960
All rights reserved
ISBN 0-472-08776-2
Library of Congress Catalog Card No. 60-7930
Published in the United States of America by
The University of Michigan Press
Manufactured in the United States of America

1997   1996   1995   1994   8   7   6   5

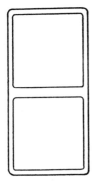

by Leslie A. White

Foreword

"The theory of cultural evolution [is] to my mind the most inane, sterile, and pernicious theory in the whole theory of science . . ." These words, by Berthold Laufer, in a review praising Lowie's *Culture and Ethnology*, fairly well expressed the point of view of the Boas group which dominated much of American anthropology for decades. Twenty-three years later, Melville J. Herskovits was "glad to affirm his belief" in an antievolutionist position (1941). And, I am told, the antievolutionist philosophy of the Boas group is still being taught in many departments of anthropology in the United States.

The repudiation of evolutionism in the United States is not easily explained. Many nonanthropological scientists find it incredible that a man who has been hailed as "the world's greatest anthropologist" (Kroeber, 1943), namely, Franz Boas, a man who was a member of the National Academy of Sciences and President of the American Association for the Advancement of Science, should have devoted himself assiduously and with vigor for decades to this antiscientific and reactionary pursuit. But it is not our purpose to attempt an explanation of this phenomenon here.

It is apparent, of course, that the foes of evolutionist theory were not liquidated with the triumph of Darwin-

v

ism in the later decades of the nineteenth century; they were merely routed for the time being and eventually regrouped their forces for a counterattack. It may be significant to also note that evolutionism flourished in cultural anthropology in a day when the capitalist system was still growing: evolution and progress were the order of the day. But when, at the close of the nineteenth century the era of colonial expansion came to an end and the capitalist-democratic system had matured and established itself securely in the Western world, then evolution was no longer a popular concept. On the contrary, the dominant note was "maintain the status quo." And, although the United States was born in armed revolt against its mother country, in mid-twentieth century it is determined that no other country shall do likewise, and the communist revolution which is spreading throughout much of the world is always called "aggression," and is opposed on moral grounds as well as with economic and military means.

As far as Boas was concerned, we would be the last to point to him as the *cause* of the antievolutionist movement in American anthropology; he was but the energetic instrument and effective catalyst of this general trend in society and ideology. As a matter of fact, one can find opposition to evolutionism on native American soil and among native-born Americans, in contrast with the German-born Boas and the largely European provenience of the prominent members of the Boas group. William James, for example, declared that "the evolutionary view of history, when it denies the vital importance of individual initiative, is, then, an utterly vague and unscientific conception, a lapse from modern scientific determinism into the most ancient oriental fatalism" (1880: 455). He also asserted that "the 'philosophy' of evolution. . . . is a metaphysical creed, and nothing else. It is a mood of contemplation, an emotional attitude, rather than a system of thought, a mood which is old as the world, and which no refutation of any one incarnation of it (such as the Spencerian philosophy) will dispell; the mood of fatalistic pantheism . . ." (*ibid.:* 458).

The case of William Jennings Bryan and the Tennessee hillbillies in the Scopes trial provides another example of native American antievolutionism outside the orbit of the Boas group.

But antievolutionism has run its course and once more the theory of evolution is on the march. Again, it may be significant to note that this is taking place in a world which is once more undergoing rapid and profound change. The so-called backward nations in Africa and Asia are rebelling against the white man and colonialism. The social organization of the whole world is undergoing profound change or is faced with this very real possibility. The status quo is fostered precariously by a nation that has assumed "world leadership."

The return to evolutionism was, of course, inevitable if progress was to continue in science and if science was to embrace cultural anthropology. The concept of evolution has proved itself to be too fundamental and fruitful to be ignored indefinitely by anything calling itself a science. Evolutionism was therefore bound to return to cultural anthropology sooner or later. The essays which follow indicate the extent to which this return has already been effected.

In addition to trends in our social and political life with their ideological repercussions, the return of evolutionism to cultural anthropology is being fostered by the Darwin Centennial. So many celebrations of the hundredth anniversary of *The Origin of Species* and the participation of so many distinguished scholars in these celebrations cannot but affect the cultural anthropologists of the United States. In comparison with the generation of McLennan, Maine, and Morgan, which placed principles above harmony and popularity, many anthropologists of today are peculiarly sensible to the opinions and regard of others; they want to be both respectable and well-liked by their fellows. We may safely predict that evolutionism in cultural anthropology will become respectable and even popular in the future. As a matter of fact, we may expect to see more than one anthropologist come forward and tell us that he has actually been an evolutionist all along. And many a would-be evolutionist will turn out to be merely a culture historian who notices similarities ("regularities") between two or more regions, or even likenesses of cause and effect in the reaction of natives to white traders (Steward, 1955, 1956). The fact that history will be mistaken for evolution, just as in the past evolution has been mistaken for history, will probably do little to dampen a new-found enthusiasm for evolutionism. But we have little to fear on this score and in the long run, however. The basic character of the concept of evolution and the sturdy and stable techniques of science will win out eventually.

Turning to the essays themselves, Sahlins' distinction between specific and general evolution should do much to clear up once and for all the long-standing confusion between history and evolution. Because an account of the evolution of a particular culture has been both chronological and specific, it has been called history. And general evolution has been termed by Kroeber "summarized history" or "merely large histories." But specific evolution is not history, an account of events that are related merely temporally and spatially. Specific evolution is still a chron-

ological sequence of forms that are functionally interrelated: one form gives rise to another. Even though confined to a single phylogenetic line, specific evolution is
still a temporal generalizing process, whereas history consists of temporal particularizing processes.

And general evolution is, if anything, even farther removed from history than specific evolution. History is
not the name of any and all kinds of temporal processes,
or an account thereof. Evolution is a temporal process
also, but of a different kind. Sahlins' distinction between
specific and general evolution should help to make it
apparent that it is the former that has often been called,
and miscalled, history; should help to make it clear that
specific evolution is just as much evolution as general
evolution. And Sahlins' treatment of general evolution
should also make it apparent that an account of the evolution of world culture, or the evolution of technology, is
not at all the same kind of thing as a historical account
of the Thirty Years' War, or any other "large history."

Sahlins' distinction between specific and general evolution should also help to end the inane debate about unilinear (or universal) evolution *vs* multilinear evolution.
No one, so far as we know, has ever maintained that the
only kind of evolution in culture was unilinear. But we
have some who argue that the only kind of valid, or
meaningful, evolutionism is multilinear (Steward, 1955;
Birdsell, 1957). As Sahlins makes perfectly clear, evolution in its specific (phylogenetic) aspect is multilinear;
evolution in its general aspect is unilinear. This distinction between the two different, but complementary and
inseparable, aspects of evolution—the unilinear and multilinear—has never been made clearer than in Sahlins'
presentation. And Sahlins makes it quite clear, too, that
general evolution is far from being "so obvious as to be

useless." On the contrary, the theory of general evolution throws a flood of light upon both whole and parts; offers an insight and an understanding that can be obtained in no other way.

It is not our purpose, nor is it our proper task, to summarize each of the chapters in this volume; each essay will speak adequately for itself and each reader will read it for himself. We may observe, however, that Harding's paper shows in an illuminating and convincing manner how the process of specific evolution may be creative in some respects but conservative in others: as the adaptive process proceeds new things are developed; but after adaptation has been achieved the emphasis is upon the status quo. In "The Law of Cultural Dominance," Kaplan distinguishes between specific dominance and general dominance. In the former, a culture, or culture type, entrenches itself in a particular environment through intensive adaptation; it persists as the type that can most effectively exploit that environment. In the case of general dominance, a type of culture is developed that has greater adaptability to a wide range of environments and a superior ability to exploit their resources. He defines The Law of Cultural Dominance in thermodynamic terms.

In his brilliant essay, "The Law of Evolutionary Potential," Service shows how this principle throws light upon and renders intelligible many anthropological problems that have remained obscure or misunderstood for a long time. His application of this law to "The Present and Future of America" is original, revealing, and positively exciting. It would do the author an injustice and the reader a disservice for me to attempt a digest or paraphrase of this part or of the whole.

Common features or characteristics of the essays are:

they are nonpsychologistic and culturological; they attempt to adhere strictly to the point of view and techniques of science, eschewing free will and other metaphysical explanatory devices; they illustrate the fundamental similarity of biological systems and cultural systems, not only from the standpoint of evolution but in other respects also; they view cultures as thermodynamic systems whose principal function is to harness free energy and put it to use.

These essays constitute the best recent treatment of cultural evolutionism that we have seen. And their excellence may be explained in part by theses which they themselves have set forth. All of the authors are younger anthropologists. A few decades ago the opponent of antievolutionism had to fight a series of propositions designed to refute evolutionist theory such as "the facts of diffusion negate evolutionism," "evolutionist theory was borrowed from biology and adapted to cultural phenomena," "the Australians had a crude technology but an advanced social system," etc. The opponent of these theories had to adapt himself to the propositions advanced by the Boasian antievolutionists and was therefore restricted in his scope and perspective. He had to develop a type of theory in opposition to specific criticisms and attacks. But these younger anthropologists have been free from such handicaps. They were not reared in the atmosphere of antievolutionism; they accepted cultural evolutionism from the very start and have therefore been relatively free from the restrictions of polemics; they have been free to explore the implications of the theory of evolution as it applies to culture and to develop its many and fruitful possibilities. And they have done it exceedingly well.

It should not be necessary to add that neither the

authors nor the present writer regard these various essays as complete, perfect, and final. They are suggestive and exploratory in some instances just as they are plausible and convincing in others. But new outlooks, fresh perspectives, and suggestions for further development of the full potentialities of cultural evolutionism are just what are needed at the present time. It is highly probable that some of the propositions set forth in this volume will be questioned; others will be challenged, perhaps with success. But this does not matter—or it will not if such criticism leads to further development and improvement instead of rejection and reaction as was the case under Boas. We believe that progress will be the result of whatever reception these essays receive. May they inspire and stimulate further work and progress along evolutionist lines so that cultural anthropology will no longer stand apart from other sciences in repudiating one of the most basic and fruitful concepts of all science.

Contents

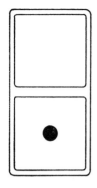

Introduction

The slenderness of this volume might seem to belie the scope of its title. We should say then at the outset that our purpose is not to describe the actual evolution of culture, but rather to argue in favor of several general principles that we believe are fundamental to the theory of cultural evolution.

An attempt of this sort is likely to meet with a somewhat more favorable reception today than it would have twenty or even ten years ago. For most of the twentieth century evolutionism has been virtually absent from British and American cultural anthropology. After an auspicious beginning in the late nineteenth century in the work of Spencer, Morgan, and Tylor, it was vigorously combated in succeeding decades by Franz Boas and his early students. It seemed for a long time that Boas had demolished evolutionism—it was "effectively exploded," one commentator put it—and since then anthropologists have not been so much actively antievolutionary as they have been indifferent, passively nonevolutionary. The arguments raised by White and Childe on behalf of the evolutionary perspective remained almost unheeded by a tranquilized generation of anthropologists.

To explain why this neglect of cultural evolution occurred would demand a lengthy and complex argument which cannot be undertaken here. Boas was the most prominent and influential of the anthropologists involved in the reaction against evolutionism, but the fact that a similar regression took place in other social sciences as well suggests that broad cultural factors were at work. This does not absolve Boas from criticism, for to cite the personal role of leading figures in the theoretical trends of a science is certainly a legitimate way to evaluate them. But it is not enough as an *explanation* of what happened.

Today, cultural evolutionism seems to be reviving. Is it because we now find ourselves observing a world-wide conflict between older, entrenched social orders and once-lowly and dominated peoples whose awakening has made "progress" again the slogan of the day? The industrial revolution and the triumph over feudalism were closely associated with the original rise of evolutionism in Western Europe; perhaps the new industrial society appearing or being sought in other parts of the world in our time is related to the current revival, the "re-enlightenment." However this may be, there are unmistakable signs of a widening interest in cultural evolution.

In British and American anthropology there has been for some years a discontent with the intellectual sterility of Boasian empiricism and its so very restricted historical concerns. The younger cultural anthropologists have seemed increasingly eager to borrow theories from any source—from sociological functionalism, from psychiatry and metaphysics, from Veblen, Weber, Marx, Freud, Toynbee, and so on—and in this eclectic atmosphere evolutionism probably can find a place.

Yet at the same time this epoch of borrowing and soul-searching that anthropology (along with some other social sciences) has entered is characterized by ephemeral intellectual fads, as Kroeber has pointed out. One may justly worry, even fear, that what may be called the "band wagon effect" is about to take place with respect to evolutionism. Thus in 1959, the centennial anniversary of the publication of the *Origin of Species*, several publications and symposia dedicated to the consideration of cultural evolutionism suddenly appeared. Certainly this is welcome, but one cannot refrain from noting the startling sea change that occurs: several prominent anthropologists who had never before evidenced an interest in evolution (other than a negative one) are now adding the word, at least, to their vocabulary. And it now appears that some of our leading anthropologists have been "doing evolution" all along (Mead 1958, for example), just as they have been speaking prose. May we say then, and as forcefully as possible, that we contest the logic of faddism: we do *not* regard the theory of evolution, and certainly not the mere word "evolution," as a universal solvent that can resolve all anthropological problems, and we do *not* think that everyone, or even anyone, should immediately give up whatever he is doing in order to stop being a "square." The evolutionary perspective had been missing in anthropology and we should like to join in current efforts toward reestablishing it, but hardly at the cost of the many other legitimate anthropological concerns.

Possibly some will identify this book with the new look, as a part of "neoevolutionism." It is as disavowal that we have written the above. Also, the book has not been inspired by, nor is it dedicated to, Charles Darwin, even though it was written in the Darwin Centennial Year. Without meaning to minimize the profound biological contributions of that great man, we should remember that the evolutionary study of society and culture long antedates him. Rather, we attempt to build on the ground plan laid out by the nineteenth-century anthropological pioneers. Our perspective is plain old evolutionary, not neoevolutionary. We take as our premise the view of E. B. Tylor, that evolution is "the great principle that every scholar must lay firm hold of, if he intends to understand either the world he lives in or the history of the past."

We accept more specifically Tylor's twofold view of the evolutionary process and of its study: on the one hand the general development through which culture as a whole has passed "stage by stage"; on the other hand the particular "evolution of culture along its many lines." An exposition of this dual nature of evolution and a discussion and resolution of the many confusions which have come about from failure to distinguish these two aspects constitute the next chapter, "Evolution: Specific and General." The third chapter, "Adaptation and Stability," examines the mechanics and consequences of the specific evolution of culture as it proceeds "along its many lines." Chapter IV, "The Law of Cultural Dominance," points up one of the great consequences of the evolution of culture in both its general and particular aspects, the rise and spread of dominant types. The fifth chapter, "The Law of Evolutionary Potential," uses the preceding conceptions, but deals with their interrelations in order to show how certain kinds of generalizations can be derived from evolutionary theory and used to interpret and predict developments in particular cases.

All of these chapters are concerned with aspects, however general, of what we conceive as the total evolutionary process. Before proceeding to them we must, then, state what we mean by evolution. It seems that there is a great deal of disagreement about this concept, especially in cultural anthropology.

4

Introduction

To some anthropologists, evolution is simply change (e.g., Birdsell 1957). To others it is growth or development, which is a special kind of change. Some would outlaw the concept of progress from evolution. Others accept "advance" but eschew the term "progress" (Greenberg 1957). Another finds progress of the very essence (White 1959). Evolution in its most significant aspect is "multilinear" we are told by one student of cultural evolution, and in its least significant aspect, "universal" (Steward 1953). It is significantly both, argue others (White 1959; Haag 1959; Kluckhohn 1959). Is evolution "history"? Most of it is, writes Kroeber, and the remainder is probably functionalism or "science" (1946). But evolution and history are distinctly different processes, White replies, and functionalism is still another (1945; 1959).

What is the relation between biological and cultural evolution? Culture is *sub specie evolutionis*, Julian Huxley asserts, a variety of evolution in general. Presumably, this implies that culture and life are "cousins," that they have common evolutionary descent. To some anthropologists this must seem a threat of reductionism—although we do not think it is—but none have as yet entered the lists against Huxley. Nevertheless, anthropology has long maintained its guard against the "biological analogy." Steward articulates this traditional position: ". . . cultural evolution is an extension of biological evolution only in a chronological sense" (1953: 313).

This book in general and the next chapter more particularly are relevant to all of these arguments. The distinction between general and specific evolution, we hope to show, will itself dissipate many of them. But behind this distinction is a certain conception of evolution.

Most definitions of evolution—whether cultural, biological, or both, is not yet relevant—are of one of two kinds. The most common calls attention to *forms* (or classes thereof) and the changes, perhaps of a particular nature, that occur in them. Forms and the succession of forms are the foci of concern. "Evolution is descent with modification" or "evolution is the succession of cultural stages" are statements of this succession-of-forms view. The second, more rarely voiced perspective conceives evolution as a grand *movement* in a certain direction and when changes in form follow that direction they are evolutionary. This perspective embraces the totality of forms, the whole of life or culture, or perhaps both and more, defining evolution by stating the direction of change of the totality. "Evolution is a movement from homogeneity to heterogeneity" is an example of the grand-movement view.

Among cultural anthropologists, Leslie White has shown the greatest theoretical concern with evolution. Although it should be noted that in considering cultural evolution itself his is a grand-movement view, holding that culture moves in the direction of increasing energy utilization, White's more philosophical discussions of evolution in general hold to succession-of-forms:

The evolutionist process is characterized by chronological sequences . . . form B follows A in time, but precedes C. The evolutionist process is concerned with form and function . . . one form grows out of, and into, another. The evolutionist process is concerned with the progression of forms through time. (1945: 229–30.)

While it is true that White applies this outlook to all reality, organic, inorganic, and superorganic, the concept "evolutionist process" itself does not specify a broad, over-all *direction* in which reality is moving. An exclusively biological definition that likewise focuses on

6

changing forms, in this case the genetic structure of populations, is the much-favored one, here voiced by Boyd, that "Evolution, essentially, is nothing but a change in gene frequencies" (1950: 131).

A grand-movement view can actually encompass and imply the succession-of-forms view. The contrast between the two and the greater inclusiveness of the former may be illustrated by a definition of Julian Huxley's: "Evolution may be regarded as the process by which the utilization of the earth's resources by living matter is rendered progressively more efficient" (1943: 387). Here the emphasis is on a total movement in which given life forms are, in a sense, the instruments or even consequences. The thermodynamic statement of evolution by Alfred Lotka is of the same grand-movement character: "Evolution proceeds in such direction as to make the total energy flux through the system [of living things] a maximum . . ." (1922: 149; cf. Lotka 1945).

Is evolution best considered as a succession-of-forms or as a sweeping movement in a certain direction? The answer to this question is governed by the reply to another: which alternative is more helpful in understanding the facts normally considered evolutionary? We suggest that a broad perspective, such as Huxley's or Lotka's, is the more fruitful. First, it helps to specify precisely the relation between biological and cultural evolution—one will be able to go beyond saying whether they are analogous or not. Secondly, it helps to draw out a distinction central to our thinking in succeeding chapters, particularly the next: that there are two kinds of evolution, or more precisely, two aspects of the total evolutionary process, specific or adaptive and general or progressive.

There is one grand movement that encompasses not only biological and cultural evolution, but presumably

7

the evolution of the universe itself: the course specified by the famous Second Law of Thermodynamics. But considered as closed systems, life and culture move in a direction different from that stipulated for the universe as a whole by the Second Law. Inorganic evolution proceeds toward decrease in organization, culminating in homogeneity and the random distribution of matter and energy. However, life and culture proceed in the opposite direction: toward increase in organization, higher energy concentration, and with a qualification to be discussed later (Chapters IV and V), toward increased heterogeneity. It is this evolution with which we are concerned.

Yet the question is naturally suggested, are not biological and cultural evolution also entirely different from each other? Obviously cultural and biological evolution do differ in many ways, for culture and life have different properties, different means of transmission and change, and each has laws peculiar to itself. Nonetheless, both can be embraced within one total view of evolution. Cultural evolution can be considered, in Huxley's phrase, *sub specie evolutionis*, a continuation, on a new line, of *the* evolutionary process.

This understanding is logical only if we accept such grand-movement perspectives on evolution as Huxley's "process by which the utilization of the earth's resources by living matter is rendered progressively more efficient." Culture is the superorganic means available to the human species for utilizing the earth's resources in the service of survival; accumulation of experience through symboling permits improvements in this endeavor: hence, cultural evolution in particular is part and continuation of evolution as a totality. The conclusion still holds if we adopt Lotka's understanding of evolution as maximi-

8

zation of the energy flux. Culture, continuing the life process, appropriates free energy and builds it into an organization for survival, and like life, culture moves to maximize the amount of energy exploitation.

It may be said that as a continuation of the evolutionary process, culture shows *more than* analogous resemblances to life, it shows homologous resemblances. ". . . there is a certain parallelism. There are strange analogies; it may be that there are homologies" (Roosevelt 1910: 7). Perhaps that is why the so-called biological analogy does not wither away in evolutionary anthropology, even in the face of many concerted and seemingly devastating intellectual attacks. The homology is primarily *functional:* both life and its offshoot, culture, are energy-capturing systems which move in the direction of thermodynamic improvement as well as adapt to various means of energy appropriation.

Homology, it is true, is normally thought of in terms of structure (morphology) not function; the fossil record of life hardly permits otherwise. Homologous structures are those which can be traced to the same origin but which have been modified differently in different species due to adaptive or functional variation. But why not also label as homologous those similarities in function traced to common descent that have been modified due to changes in structure? The functional similarities of life and culture are cognatic, products of their common evolutionary descent.

The value of conceiving cultural and biological evolution as homologous is that it provides a sound rationale for students of each to examine the others' findings. This is the heuristic value of recognizing any homology, structural or functional. Theoretically, if we know a great deal about the limb structure and functioning in one kind of animal and little about the homologous aspects of a related one, consideration of the first would help us to understand the second. Similarly, knowledge of the characteristics of general progress in culture can breed knowledge about comparable aspects of life, or vice versa. By definition the things compared are not identical; hence, conclusions drawn about one are not necessarily relevant to the other. But if they are homologous it follows that insofar as similarities are observed in the things studied, the probability is that these similarities can be explained in similar terms. To explain two things in similar terms is not the same as explaining one in terms of the other. Therefore there is no reductionism.

In fact, recognition of the homologous aspects of biological and cultural evolution has long been implicit in evolutionary anthropology and in its terminology, even among those such as Steward who explicitly disavow the biological analogy. What else can better justify the use of such terms and ideas as "adaptation," "specialization," "ecology" and the like in both anthropology and biology? Undoubtedly, there will be other-minded anthropologists who reject this general reasoning, if not the terms in particular. Perhaps the objections of some can be overcome by pointing out that many connotations of "structure" and "function," terms so very popular now, have intruded into anthropology from the same source as these evolutionary ideas. Should we throw out "structural-functionalism" as a biological analogy? At any rate, it will not do to reject the conclusions of this book a priori on such grounds, or just because "biological analogy" has so long been a pejorative term for almost anything regarding cultural evolution that it has attained the status of an antievolutionary tropism.

The grand-movement view of evolution, stated in

either Huxley's or Lotka's terms, is accepted here along with its implication of homologous resemblance between the cultural and biological phases of the total movement. In both these phases the dual character of the evolutionary process, specific adaptation and general progress, can be observed. The distinction between the specific-adaptive and the general-progressive aspects of evolution may be introduced by quoting Julian Huxley's invidious comparison between the presumably lamentable condition of evolutionary anthropology and the supposedly sophisticated status of evolutionary biology:

When anthropologists realize the fact that evolution always involves divergence as well as advance, stabilization as well as improvement, and when they have reached a fuller understanding of the mechanisms of cultural maintenance, transmission, and transformation, we may reasonably forecast a broadly similar course for anthropology, including the prospect of an eventual triumphant synthesis. (1956: 15.)

We are not presuming to offer a "triumphant synthesis." But we do seek to make explicit that for culture, as for life, evolution involves "advance" as well as "divergence," over-all progress as well as variation. It is these two aspects that are labelled General Evolution and Specific Evolution respectively.

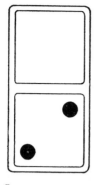 *Evolution: Specific and General*

It seems to us that Huxley has been premature in congratulating evolutionary biology on its explicit recognition of the difference between divergence and progress. Despite Huxley's own efforts to make the distinction, and despite the fact that the distinction may well strike a biologist as commonplace should he pause to consider it, it is nevertheless not generally explicated by prominent biologists, and judging from confusion about the character of life's evolutionary progress in recent literature (e.g., Simpson 1950: Chapter XV), it is perhaps not fully understood. On the other hand, the distinction has long existed in the literature of evolutionary anthropology. E. B. Tylor, in the opening chapter of *Primitive Culture* (1871), laid out the study of cultural evolution both "stage by stage" as well as "along its many lines." Yet in this, as in so much else, twentieth-century anthropology did not heed Tylor's advice. The dual character of the evolutionary process was not recognized, and this failing has become the very heart of current confusion and polemical controversy about such terms as "unilinear," "multilinear," and "universal" evolution, as well as about the difference between "history" and "evolution."

It appears almost obvious upon stating it that in both its biological and cultural spheres evolution moves simultaneously in two directions. On one side, it creates diversity through adaptive modification: new forms differentiate from old. On the other side, evolution generates progress: higher forms arise from, and surpass, lower. The first of these directions is Specific Evolution, and the second, General Evolution. But note that specific and general evolution are not different concrete realities; they are rather aspects of the same total process, which is also to say, two contexts in which we may place the same evolutionary things and events. Any given change in a form of life or culture can be viewed *either* in the perspective of adaptation *or* from the point of view of overall progress. However, the context is very important: a difference in taxonomy is required in examining these two aspects of evolution. Concerned with lines of descent, the study of specific evolution employs phylogenetic classification. In the general evolutionary outlook emphasis shifts to the character of progress itself, and forms are classed in stages or levels of development without reference to phylogeny.

SPECIFIC AND GENERAL BIOLOGICAL EVOLUTION

Life inevitably diversifies. It does so because it is perpetuated by reproduction and inheritance, so that adaptive changes are transmitted only in lines of descent. Thus in evolving—which is to say, moving in the direction of increasing use of the earth's resources or increasing transformation of available energy—life necessarily differentiates into particular (breeding) populations, each adjusted to the exploitation of a given environment. This is the specific aspect of life's evolution, the familiar origin and ramification of species. The much-lauded "modern synthetic theory" of biology, unifying genetic principles with natural selection, is devoted to the unraveling of specific evolution.

13

The perspective required for understanding specific evolution is a phylogenetic one. We are interested in how one species grows out of another and how the new species gives rise to still other species. We are interested in the precise historical and genetic relations between species, and want to show these connections as well as to explain them by reference to natural selection. Thus we trace out the branching and rebranching of lineages, relating each new line to its ecological circumstances. Inasmuch as our perspective is phylogenetic, so is our taxonomy. While biological taxonomy was not originally phylogenetic, it has come to be primarily so used, indicating again that the decisive concern of evolutionary biology remains specific evolution.

Adaptive specialization of populations is an inevitable aspect of life's evolution, and *advance* is a normal concomitant of adaptive specialization. In the context of specific evolution "advance" means that by adaptive modification the population is enabled to maintain or better itself in the face of a threat induced by changing environment or that it is enabled to exploit the same environment more effectively than before. In any case, in the specific perspective advance is characteristically *relative*—relative to the environmental circumstances. This can be illustrated by looking at adapting species in terms of structure and functioning.

Specific advance is manifest both in improved structure and improved functioning of members of an adapting population, although improved structure usually receives greater attention because it is more easily observed or (for fossils) deduced. There are many possible kinds of functional improvements: in vision, smell, speed, or in temperature control, and so on. Likewise there are many possible kinds of concomitant structural improvements:

14

changes in limb structure, in the brain, in the eyes, the development of claws, fins, fur, and the like. But that which is a significant improvement for one species need not be so for another, for they may be adjusting to radically different environments or in radically different ways to the same kind of environment. For some forms in some habitats, increase in size is an adaptive advance, for others, decrease in size is selectively advantageous, and so with all other characteristics. Therefore, no one organism, however high in general standing, has a monopoly on or even necessarily more kinds of adaptive advances than any other. A "higher species," in other words, is not in every respect more "advanced" than a lower: man's color vision may be superior to that of the fish, but he cannot swim as well, nor for that matter is his eyesight the most perfect in the animal kingdom. Moreover, higher organisms are not inevitably more perfectly adjusted to their environments than lower. On the contrary, many higher species die out while lower forms continue to survive in their particular niches for eons. Higher forms are often more generalized, less specialized (adapted) for any particular niche, than lower.

Adaptive improvement is relative to the adaptive problem; it is so to be judged and explained. In the specific context each adapted population is adequate, indeed superior, in its own incomparable way. Considering life's evolution phylogenetically we can be only biological relativists. At this point the cultural anthropologist will probably be unable to refrain from linking the famous axiom of cultural relativism with a specific perspective on cultural change. Such would be a correct historical inference: the philosophy of cultural relativism was elaborated precisely by the historical-particularist school which dominated American anthropology through the first half of this century. But to pursue this further now is to anticipate a later discussion.

In sum, specific evolution is the phylogenetic, adaptive, diversifying, specializing, ramifying aspect of total evolution. It is in this respect that evolution is often equated with movement from homogeneity to heterogeneity. But general evolution is another aspect. It is the emergence of higher forms of life, regardless of particular lines of descent or historical sequences of adaptive modification. In the broader perspective of general evolution organisms are taken out of their respective lineages and grouped into types which represent the successive levels of all-round progress that evolution has brought forth.

Let us first illustrate the difference between general and specific evolution with a diagram (Diagram 1). Suppose it is possible to plot the phylogenetic origins of the major lineages of animal life. A good way of doing this graphically would be in the shape of a climbing vine— not a tree, for there is no trunk, no "main line"—each larger branch of the vine representing a major divergence of life through time, and smaller branches representing diversification of major lineages. But the vine has a dimension of height as well as a temporal extension of branches. Suppose that the height is "evolutionary height," that is, that the distance of any form from the base indicates degree of over-all progress according to some agreed-upon criterion. A series of horizontal lines could then be drawn across the vine, with the vertical intervals between them indicating levels of general progress through time. Thus on the diagram, life's evolution is depicted in its lateral, branching dimension as well as in its vertical, progressive one.

The difference between specific and general evolution can also be illustrated by reference to a familiar group

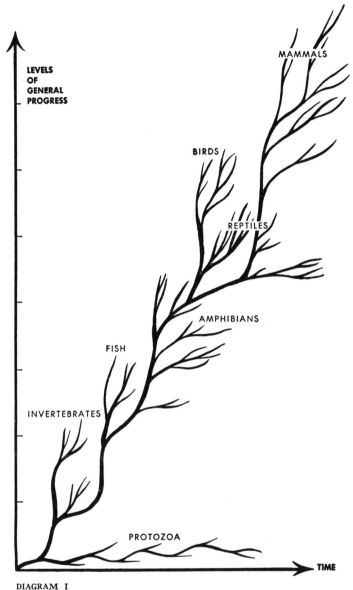

DIAGRAM I

Diversity and progress among major lineages
of animal life (schematized).

of animals, the primates. The primates are customarily divided into four broad formal categories: prosimian, New World monkeys, Old World monkeys, and hominoid. Each of the latter three, according to Simpson (1950), originated from a different line of prosimian, not one developed out of another. Phylogenetically or specifically, the study of primates consists of tracing the early prosimian radiation, determining how, when, and why each of the other types specialized out, and following the further course of divergence within each line. But it seems obvious and is usually implicitly accepted that the four types of primates, especially their recent representatives, can be arranged to indicate levels of general progress. The hierarchy of over-all standing is, of course: prosimian, New World monkey, then Old World monkey, with hominoid as highest. Although the sequence is a violation of phylogeny, it aids in understanding other consequences of evolution. The hierarchy is commonly used to illustrate general progress in intelligence, social life, and a number of other features. Moreover, a check of history reveals that the levels represented by selected recent specimens are indeed successive. The implication of the last statement deserves to be made explicit: in the taxonomy of general evolution a modern representative of a stage is as "good," i.e., as indicative of the level, as the original and probably extinct representative.

As with the primates, so with life forms in general: a man is more highly developed than a mouse, a mouse than a lizard, a lizard than a goldfish, a goldfish than a crab, a crab than an amoeba. All of these are contemporary, no one is ancestral to the other; they are present termini of different lineages. In what sense can we speak of evolutionary development of one over the other? To anticipate

18

again, the same question appears when we look at contemporary cultures. Eskimo, Sioux Indian, and English culture all exist at the same time and are unrelated to each other. What are the criteria for deciding which is higher on the evolutionary scale, and which lower?

Before an answer can be suggested, another distinction is required. Anyone will recognize the taxonomic shift that occurs in moving from specific to general evolution, a shift from phylogenetic categories to levels of development respectively. But another more subtle shift has also occurred: that is, from species or populations as such to particular organisms as such. In specific evolution the unit of study is the population, the species as a whole, which evolves or differentiates into new kinds of populations. The well-known biological definition of specific evolution, a change in gene frequencies, is a statement explicitly about the structure of a population. In moving to general evolution, however, the concern becomes forms *qua* forms, typical organisms of a class and *their* characteristics. The general taxonomic category, the level, refers to a class of organisms of a given type. It is accurate to say that specific evolution is the production of diverse species, general evolution the production of higher forms.

The difference is not a semantic nicety; it becomes decisive for determining criteria of general progress. It must be recognized that the evolutionary success of a species is often accomplished at the expense of higher development of its individuals. In many situations a species is better maintained by utilizing available energy to produce more of its kind rather than a smaller number of more highly developed specimens (something like modern "higher" education). Specific and general evolution can thus be at cross-purposes, and a measure of the success of a species is not necessarily one of the degree of general development of the particular organisms involved.

Now to a most important point: to embrace general evolution is to abandon relativism. The study of all-round progress requires criteria that are absolute, that are relevant to all organisms regardless of particular environments. The development of higher organisms can be conceived in functional, energy-capturing terms: higher forms harness more energy than lower. Or the criteria of general progress may be structural, the achievement of higher organization.

One common notion of progress can be dismissed out of hand. Most of us have a tendency to equate progress with *efficiency*, which is not altogether surprising because this idea is peculiarly appropriate to a competitive, free-enterprise economy. But an organism's thermodynamic efficiency is not a measure of its general evolutionary status. By efficiency we usually mean some ratio of output to input; thus in rating a machine's efficiency we divide the output of work by the input of energy. Analogously, a measure of the thermodynamic efficiency of a living thing would be the amount of energy captured and used relative to the organism's own expenditure in the process of taking it. But suppose we know the efficiency of an organism as an energy-capturing machine; the use to which the efficiency is put remains unknown. Is it put into build-up and maintenance of its organization? Not necessarily. As pointed out before, the energy taken can be put into the build-up of higher structures *or* into more numerous offspring, each of which concentrates a relatively low amount of energy. The implication is inescapable: an organism can be more efficient than another and yet remain less highly developed.

The difference between higher and lower life forms, it seems to us, is not how efficiently energy is harnessed, but how much. Thermodynamic achievement is the ability to concentrate energy in the organism, to put energy to work building and maintaining structure. Living things take free energy from nature, use it, and dissipate it. In the long run dissipation equals capture, or in terms of entropy, exceeds it—the entropy in the environment in which an organism has lived and died is greater after than before the process. But while alive the organism is trapping energy and transforming it into a higher state, that of protoplasm and its upkeep. It is the amount so trapped (corrected for gross size of the form) and the degree to which it is raised to a higher state that would seem to be the evolutionary measure of life; that would seem to be the way that a crab is superior to an amoeba, a goldfish to a crab, a mouse to a goldfish, a man to a mouse. We put all this in quite qualified form because we lack any competence in physical biology, and do not know how to specify the operations required to ascertain this measure. "A man's reach should exceed his grasp."

But the ability to calculate general progress hardly need remain limited because of our ignorance. General progress can be stated in other, more well-known terms: in terms of organization. Thermodynamic accomplishment has its structural concomitant, greater organization. The relation between energy-harnessing and organization is reciprocal: the more energy concentrated the greater the structure, and the more complicated the structure the more energy that can be harnessed. What is meant by "greater," "higher," or "more complicated" organization? The connotations of these terms are embraced within another, even more formidable one: "level of integration."

The idea of level of integration can be broken down into three aspects. An organism is at a higher level of integration than another when it has more parts and sub-parts (a higher order of segmentation); when its parts are more specialized; and when the whole is more effectively integrated. Thus general progress in life proceeds in the development of specialized organs and organic sub-systems, such as digestive, respiratory, reproductive, and the like, and also in the development of special mechanisms of integration, such as the central nervous system and the brain. When organisms are compared on this basis, over-all progress is clearly seen in the evolutionary record.

And there are still other yardsticks of life's general progress. These are again functional but not put thermodynamically. Huxley's phrase, "all-round adaptability," sums them up. Higher organisms are freer from environmental control than lower, or more precisely, they adapt to a greater variety of particular environments while less bound to any limited niche. It may be that this can also be expressed in terms of greater mobility: higher forms have more, and more complex, motions than lower. More developed organisms are more intelligent also, which is perhaps again only another way of saying that they have more complex motions. Finally, and related to all these aspects of all-round adaptability, higher forms have greater dominance ranges than less developed types.

To recapitulate: specific evolution is "descent with modification," the adaptive variation of life "along its many lines"; general evolution is the progressive emergence of higher life "stage by stage." The advance or improvement we see in specific evolution is relative to the adaptive problem; it is progress in the sense of progression along a line from one point to another, from less to more adjusted to a given habitat. The progress of general evolution is, in contrast, absolute; it is passage from less to greater energy exploitation, lower to higher levels of integration, and less to greater all-round adaptability. Viewing evolution in its specific context, our perspective and taxonomy is phylogenetic, but the taxonomy of general evolution crosscuts lineages, grouping forms into stages of over-all development.

SPECIFIC AND GENERAL CULTURAL EVOLUTION

Culture continues the evolutionary process by new means. Since these cultural means are unique, cultural evolution takes on distinctive characteristics. But still culture diversifies by adaptive specialization and still it successively produces over-all higher forms. Culture, like life, undergoes specific and general evolution.

The cultural anthropologist surveying the ethnographic and archaeological achievements of his discipline is confronted by variety if nothing else. There are myriads of culture types, that is, of the culture characteristic of an ethnic group or a region, and an even greater variety of cultures proper, of the cultural organization of given cohesive societies. How has this come about? In a word, through adaptive modification: culture has diversified as it has filled in the variety of opportunities for human existence afforded by the earth. Such is the specific aspect of cultural evolution. One of the best statements it has received belongs to Herbert Spencer, who, ironically, is commonly and pejoratively categorized today as a "unilinear" evolutionist.

Like other kinds of progress, social progress is not linear but divergent and re-divergent. Each differentiated product gives origin to a new set of differentiated products. While spreading over the earth mankind have found environments of various characters, and in each case the social life fallen into, partly determined by the social life previously led, has been partly determined by the influences of the new environment; so that multiplying groups have tended ever to acquire differences, now major and now minor: there have arisen genera and species of societies. (1897: 3, 331.)

That culture is man's means of adaptation is a commonplace. Culture provides the technology for appropriating nature's energy and putting it to service, as well as the social and ideological means of implementing the process. Economically, politically, and in other ways, a culture also adjusts to the other cultures of its milieu, to the superorganic part of its environment. (See the important discussion of this point in the next chapter.) Cultures are organizations for doing something, for perpetuating human life and themselves. Logically as well as empirically, it follows that as the problems of survival vary, cultures accordingly change, that culture undergoes phylogenetic, adaptive development.

The raw materials of a culture's phylogenetic development are the available culture traits, both those within the culture itself and those that can be borrowed or appropriated from its superorganic environment. The orienting process of development is adaptation of these traits to the expropriation of nature's resources and to coping with outside cultural influence. In this orienting, adaptive process elements within a culture are synthesized to form new traits, an event we call "invention," and items made available from the outside are incorporated, a process we call "diffusion," or sometimes, "acculturation."

It is time we took stock of the specific evolutionary sophistication of our discipline. The culturological study of the mechanics of invention, diffusion, and cultural adaptation in general—including cultural ecology (cf.

Steward 1955)—is fairly well advanced. We need not bow before Huxley's invidious comparison of our understanding of cultural evolution and the "triumphant synthesis" of (specific) evolutionary biology. The synthesis exists in anthropology; it remains only to make it intellectually triumphant.

New cultural traits arising through adaptation can be considered adaptive advances. In this they are similar to structural and functional advances in species, although they are quite different in content. A cultural advance may appear as an innovation in kin reckoning, a "Dionysian" war complex, the elaboration of head-hunting, the development or the redefinition of the concept of mana, or any of a host of other things. Even an efflorescence of stone statuary can be viewed in an adaptive context (among others), as we suggested recently for the stone heads of Easter Island:

The earliest Easter Islanders arrived from the central Polynesian hearth with a ramage organization [in Fried's (1957) terms, "ranked lineages"] and a tradition of image carving. The organization was suited to and reinforced by communal labor and specialized production [in utilitarian spheres]. Environmental features of the new home largely precluded the use of communal and specialist labor in subsistence production. As a result, these efforts were channelled into an esoteric domain of culture. Perhaps facilitated by a tradition of carving, a limited amount of wood [yet] the availability of easily worked tuff, the canalization toward esoteric production took the particular direction that resulted in the renowned stone heads of Easter Island. (Sahlins 1955: 1051.)

To cite further examples is unnecessary: recent years have witnessed an abundance of studies demonstrating that special cultural features arise in the process of adaptation. This is the kind of work in which Julian Steward has pioneered.

We are, unfortunately, still accustomed to speak of cultural adaptive modifications such as Easter Island stone images—or Australian section systems, Eskimo technical ingenuity, Northwest Coast potlatching, or Paleolithic cave art—as "cultural bents," manifestations of "cultural interest" or "cultural outlook." But to what purpose? Our understanding has not been enhanced (as usual) by restatement in anthropomorphic terms. In the evolutionary perspective these "bents" are adaptive specializations. So considered they can be interpreted in relation to selective pressures and the available means of maintaining a cultural organization given such pressures (see Chapter III).

Adaptive advance is relative to the adaptive problem. In this context a Grecian urn is not a thing of beauty and a joy forever: it is not higher, or better, than a Chinese vase or a Hopi pot; among languages, suffixing tendencies are not more advanced than prefixing; Eskimo kin terminology is no higher than Crow; neither Eskimo nor Crow culture is more developed than the other. *Viewed specifically*, the adaptive modifications occurring in different historical circumstances are incomparable; each is adequate in its own way, given the adaptive problems confronted and the available means of meeting them. No one culture has a monopoly on or even necessarily more kinds of adaptive improvements, and what is selectively advantageous for one may be simply ruinous for another. Nor are those cultures that we might consider higher in general evolutionary standing necessarily more perfectly adapted to their environments than lower. Many great civilizations have fallen in the last 2,000 years, even in the midst of material plenty, while the Eskimos tenaciously maintained themselves in an incomparably more difficult habitat. The race is not to the swift, nor the battle to the strong.

When we look at the specific aspect of culture's evolution we are cultural relativists. But this is not justification for the extension or the distortion of the relativist injunction that says "progress" is only a moral judgment, and all "progress," like all morality, is therefore only relative. Adaptive advances considered as such are relative. Like morals they are to be judged as more or less effective specializations. But general progress also occurs in culture, and it can be absolutely, objectively, and nonmoralistically ascertained.

So far specific cultural evolution has been treated much like specific biological evolution, often in identical terms; but there are also important differences. The fundamental differences stem from the fact that cultural variation, unlike biological, can be transmitted between different lines by diffusion. Separate cultural traditions, unlike separate biological lineages, may converge by coalescence. Moreover, partial phylogenetic continuity sometimes occurs between successive general stages of cultural evolution as backward cultures, borrowing wholesale the achievements of higher forms, push on to new evolutionary heights without recapitulating all intermediate stages of development. By contrast, each new adaptive step is a point of no return for biological populations; they can only (at best) move forward to that full specialization which is ultimately the (dead) end of further progress. In the same connection, replacement of a less highly developed by a more progressive cultural form can be accomplished by diffusion or acculturation, which has the advantage for people that a higher culture may dominate without total destruction of the population, or even loss of ethnic or social integrity, of the lower. In the chapters to follow these unique qualities of cultural evolution are examined in detail.

While convergence by diffusion is common in specific cultural evolution, so is parallel independent development, as anthropology has learned well after years of controversy over "diffusion versus independent invention." Perhaps parallel, independent development—the consequence of similar adaptation to similar environment—is more common in culture than comparable phenomena seem to be in life because of the limitation on variation imposed by the generic similarity and unity of humanity, the "psychic unity of mankind." In any case, a professional anthropologist can immediately bring to mind a host of parallelisms or "regularities," as Steward calls them, in cultural evolution. Steward, incidentally, virtually equates parallelism with his term, "multilinear evolution," and, furthermore, asserts that multilinear evolution is anthropology's only road to profitable, albeit limited, evolutionary generalization (Steward 1953; 1955). We have something to say about this in the concluding section of the chapter.

Specific evolution is not the whole of cultural evolution. Culture not only produces adaptive sequences of forms, but sequences of higher forms; it has not only undergone phylogenetic development, but over-all progress. In brief, culture has evolved in a general respect as well as a specific one.

General cultural evolution is the successive emergence of new levels of all-round development. This emergent process, however, is not necessarily a historically continuous, phylogenetic one, for new levels of general standing are often achieved in unconnected (or only partially connected) cultural traditions. The relation between general and specific cultural evolution can thus be depicted as we have done before for comparable aspects of biological evolution. *Mutatis mutandis*, Diagram 1 (p. 17) will serve for both—with the proviso that various culture lines may cross at many points to indicate convergence by diffusion.

The general perspective on cultural evolution has been labelled, by its critics, "universal evolution." Readers other than anthropologists may find this difficult to believe, but the very term "universal" has a negative connotation in this field because it suggests the search for broad generalization that has been virtually declared unscientific (!) by twentieth-century, academic, particularistic American anthropology. Correlatively, "universal evolution" is criticized on the grounds that it *is* universal, i.e., so general as to be vague, obvious, or simply truistic (e.g., Steward 1955). We hope the reader, then, will pardon us for a rather long digression concerning the scientific value of the study of general evolution.

The objectives of general evolutionary research are the determination and explanation of the successive transformations of culture through its several stages of overall progress. What progressive trends have emerged in warfare, for example, or in economy, in political institutions, or in the role of kinship in society? As the questions we ask are not posed in terms of adaptive modification, neither will our explanations be. In other words, studies of specific and general evolution lead in different directions, as has evolution itself.

Let us take for an example the evolutionary analysis of war. Considered phylogenetically or specifically, variations in warfare are related to the selective circumstances operating on the cultures involved. In this way we examine and explain the development of warfare among Plains Indians in the nineteenth century (see, for example, Secoy 1953), or why it differs from war among California Indians or the Iroquois. Each type of warfare thus considered is a unique, historic type, to be interpreted with reference to its particular historical-ecological circumstances. Using a general perspective, however, we classify types of warfare as representatives of stages in the over-all development of that aspect of culture, and then trace the progressive trends in war as they unfold through these successive stages. (Incidentally, anyone can see from the example we have chosen that "progress" is not here equated with "good.") The progressive trends discovered might include such things as increase in the scale of war, in the size of armies and the numbers of casualties, in the duration of campaigns, and the significance of outcome for the survival of the societies involved. These trends find their explanation not in adaptation but by reference to other developments accompanying them in the general progress of culture, such as increasing economic productivity or the emergence of special political institutions. Our conclusions now are of the form: war changes in certain ways, such as increases in scale, duration, etc., in proportion to certain economic or political (or whatever) trends, such as increasing productivity. It is obvious that the evolution of war has involved both diversification and progressive development, and only the employment of both specific and general perspectives can confront the evolutionary whole.

Distinguishing diversification from progress, however, not only distinguishes kinds of evolutionary research and conclusions, it dissipates long-standing misconceptions. Here is a question typical of a whole range of such difficulties: is feudalism a general *stage* in the evolution of economic and political forms, the one antecedent to modern national economy? The affirmative has virtually been taken for granted in economic and political history, and not only of the Marxist variety, where the sequence slave-feudal-capitalist modes of production originated. If assumed to be true, then the unilineal implications of the evolutionary scheme are only logical. That is, if feudalism is the antecedent stage of the modern state, then it, along with "Middle Ages" and "natural economy," lies somewhere in the background of every modern civilization. So it is that in the discipline of history, the Near East, China, Japan, Africa, and a number of other places have been generously granted "Middle Ages."

But it is obvious nonsense to consider feudalism, Middle Ages, and natural economy as the *general stage* of evolution antecedent to high (modern) civilization. Many civilizations of antiquity that antedate feudalism in its classic European form, as well as some coeval and some later than it in other parts of the world, are more highly developed. Placing feudalism between these civilizations and modern nations in a hierarchy of over-all progress patently and unnecessarily invalidates the hierarchy; it obscures rather than illustrates the progressive trends in economy, society, and polity in the evolution of culture. Conversely, identifying the specific antecedents of modern civilizations throughout the world as "feudalism" is also obviously fallacious and obscures the historic course of development of these civilizations, however much it may illuminate the historic course of Western culture.

Is not Marx [in the *Communist Manifesto*] in reality beginning with an analysis of the social development of Western Europe and the countries brought from time to time within its orbit from the Dark Ages to the growth of an advanced system of Capitalism, and then trying to apply the results achieved by this analysis to human history as a whole? May not the first of these steps be valid, and the second invalid . . . Were the Dark Ages really an advance over the Roman Empire? Civilisation for civilisation, can anyone possibly believe that they were? (Cole 1934: 38–39.)

Feudalism is a "stage" only in a *specific* sense, a step in the development of one line of civilization. The stage of general evolution achieved prior to the modern nation is best represented by such classical civilizations as the Roman, or by such oriental states as China, Sumer, and the Inca Empire. In the general perspective, feudalism is only a specific, backward form of this order of civilization, an underdeveloped form that happened to have greater evolutionary potential than the others and historically gave rise to a new level of achievement. As Chapter V will show, there is nothing unusual in evolutionary "leapfrogging" of this sort. The failure to differentiate these general and specific facets of the development of civilization can only be a plague on both houses of evolutionary research and a disgrace to the whole evolutionary perspective.

The reader may well feel disturbed, if not deceived, by the preceding discussion. How can an exposition of the course of evolution arbitrarily rip cultures out of the context of time and history and place them, just as arbitrarily, in categories of lower and higher development, categories that are presumed to represent *successive* stages? We are confronting the taxonomic innovation that is required for the study of general evolution.

Perhaps it will help to point out that in biological evolution new forms of low degree are arising all the time, such as new forms of bacteria; in other words, the specific evolution of lower forms does not stop when they are by-passed by higher forms. It follows that the later form is not necessarily higher than the earlier; the *stages* or *levels* of general development are successive, but the particular representatives of successive stages need not be. To return to feudalism, it represents a lower level of general development than the civilizations of China, ancient Egypt, or Mesopotamia, although it arose later than these civilizations and happened to lead to a form still higher than any of them.

The fundamental difference between specific and general evolution appears in this: the former is a connected, historic sequence of forms, the latter a sequence of stages exemplified by forms of a given order of development. In general evolutionary classification, any representative of a given cultural stage is inherently as good as any other, whether the representative be contemporaneous and ethnographic or only archaeological. The assertion is strengthened very much by the knowledge that there is a generic relation between the technical subsystem of a culture and the social and philosophical subsystems, so that a contemporaneous primitive culture with a given technology is equivalent, for general purposes, to certain extinct ones known only by the remains of a similar technology.

The *unit* of general evolutionary taxonomy, it should be noted, is a cultural system proper, that is, the cultural organization of a sociopolitical entity. A *level* of general development is a class of cultures of a given order. But what are the criteria for placing particular cultures in such classes, for deciding which is higher and which lower?

In culture, as in life, thermodynamic accomplishment is fundamental to progress, and therefore would appear useful as a criterion of emergent development. It is well known that revolutionary all-round advance occurs when and where new sources of energy are tapped, or major technological improvements are applied to already available sources (White 1959). But here we enter a caveat similar to that brought up in connection with the thermodynamic development of life: general progress is not to be equated with thermodynamic *efficiency*.

Technological innovation can raise efficiency, i.e., increase the amount of energy captured per unit of human energy expended, yet still not stimulate the progressive development of a culture. Whether or not, or to what extent, a gain in productive efficiency is actually employed in the build-up and maintenance of higher organization depends on local selective circumstances. An increase in efficiency may not be directed toward any advance whatsoever if the existing adaptation cannot accommodate it or the selective pressures remain insufficient to induce it. A people may adopt a technological innovation that theoretically might double output, but instead, they only work half as long (twice as efficiently) as they used to. Such, indeed, is a common outcome of the imposition, however "well-meaning," of Western technology the world over. Or, as Harris has pointed out (1959), a gain in efficiency can as well be put into increasing population as into more goods and services, means of communication, new political systems, or the promulgation of transcendental philosophies, and so forth. A continuation on this course will eventually lead to an expansion of population beyond available social means of organizing it. In an open environment the society will fission into two or more societies, each at a relatively low level of cultural organization, rather than producing one cultural system of a high order of development. Progress is not the inevitable outcome of efficiency.

Evolution: Specific and General

It seems to us that progress is the total transformation of energy involved in the creation and perpetuation of a cultural organization. A culture harnesses and delivers energy; it extracts energy from nature and transforms it into people, material goods, and work, into political systems and the generation of ideas, into social customs and into adherence to them. The total energy so transformed from the free to the cultural state, in combination perhaps with the degree to which it is raised in the transformation (the loss in entropy), may represent a culture's general standing, a measure of its achievement.

The reader will surmise from the qualified phraseology that we are once more on uncertain ground. It is hardly consolation that we share this unenviable position with our colleagues; it does not appear that any satisfactory and usable method of quantifying the thermodynamic achievements of different cultures has been developed—or even that, with a few exceptions, anyone is very much concerned. Perhaps a start can be made by estimating the total mechanical energy delivered per year by a society. Among primitives, where human beings are usually the sole form of mechanical energy, the calculation would be relatively simple: population size multiplied by average manpower (in energy units) over the year. In societies using nonhuman mechanical energy as well as human, the two are added together—statistics of the amount of nonhuman mechanical energy of many modern societies are available.

Although there is a lack, for the moment, of ready estimations of cultural progress in energy terms, the attempt to measure general standing need by no means be abandoned. There are good structural criteria. As in life, thermodynamic achievement has its organizational counterpart, higher levels of integration. Cultures that

35

transform more energy have more parts and subsystems, more specialization of parts, and more effective means of integration of the whole. Organizational symptoms of general progress include the proliferation of material elements, geometric increase in the division of labor, multiplication of social groups and subgroups, and the emergence of special means of integration: political, such as chieftainship and the state, and philosophical, such as universal ethical religions and science. Long ago, Spencer described all this in painstaking, if not always accurate, detail. Although many social scientists deny that the idea of "progress" is applicable to culture, how can it be denied in the terms we have just stated it? As Greenberg remarks —despite the fact that he rejects the term "progress," after having defined it morally—a theory

. . . which regarded all species as interconnected but which posited some mammalian form as the primeval ancestral type, whence descended in one line all the other vertebrates, in another the ancestor of all non-vertebrate phyla, with Protozoa first appearing in a very recent period, would not be adjudged a representative evolutionary theory. (1957: 58–59.)

Similarly, culture has not fallen from evolutionary heights; it has risen to them.

The social subsystem of cultures is especially illustrative of progress in organization, and it is often used to ascertain general evolutionary standing. The traditional and fundamental division of culture into two great stages, primitive and civilized, is usually recognized as a social distinction: the emergence of a special means of integration, the state, separates civilization from primitive society organized by kinship. Within the levels *societas* and *civitas*, moreover, further stages can be discriminated on

36

criteria of social segmentation and integration. On the primitive level, the unsegmented (except for families) and chiefless *bands* are least advanced—and characteristically, preagricultural. More highly developed are agricultural and pastoral tribes segmented into clans, lineages, and the like, although lacking strong chiefs. Higher than such egalitarian *tribes*, and based on greater productivity, are *chiefdoms* with internal status differentiation and developed chieftainship. Similarly, within the level of civilization we can distinguish the *archaic* form—characteristically ethnically diverse and lacking firm integration of the rural, peasant sector—from the more highly developed, more territorially and culturally integrated *nation state*, with its industrial technology.

General progress can also be viewed as improvement in "all-round adaptability." Higher cultural forms tend to dominate and replace lower, and the range of dominance is proportionate to the degree of progress. So modern national culture tends to spread around the globe, before our eyes replacing, transforming, and extinguishing representatives of millennia-old stages of evolution, while archaic civilization, now also falling before this advance, even in its day was confined to certain sectors of certain of the continents. The dominance power of higher cultural forms is a consequence of their ability to exploit greater ranges of energy resources more effectively than lower forms. Higher forms are again relatively "free from environmental control," i.e., they adapt to greater environmental variety than lower forms. (See the discussion of dominance in Chapter IV. By way of aside, the human participants in this process typically articulate the increasing all-round adaptability of higher civilizations as increase in their *own* powers: the more energy and habitats culture masters, the more man becomes convinced of his own control of destiny and the more he seems to proclaim his anthropocentric view of the whole cultural process. In the past we humbly explained our limited success as a gift of the gods: we were *chosen* people; now we are *choosing* people.)

General cultural evolution, to summarize, is passage from less to greater energy transformation, lower to higher levels of integration, and less to greater all-round adaptability. Specific evolution is the phylogenetic, ramifying, historic passage of culture along its many lines, the adaptive modification of particular cultures.

SOME IMPLICATIONS

We should now like to relate the distinction drawn between specific and general evolution to current scholarly views of evolution, particularly to anthropological views.

But first a word about terms: "specific evolution" and "general evolution" are probably not the best possible labels for the adaptive and over-all progressive aspects of the evolutionary process. Friends and colleagues have suggested others: "lineal," "adaptive," "special," "particular," and "divergent" have been offered for "specific"; "emergent," "progressive," or "universal" for "general." All the alternatives we judge to be somewhat inadequate, for one reason or another, although some were occasionally used in the preceding discussion. In a recent publication, Greenberg (1959) distinguishes "transformism" from "advance" in evolution, which seems to correspond to our "specific" and "general." The reader is free to adopt any of the alternatives. The terms are not the issue; the issue is empirical realities.

. . . when we define a word we are merely inviting others to use it as we would like it to be used . . . the purpose of definition is to focus argument upon fact, and . . . the proper result of good definition is to transform argument over terms into disagreements about fact, and thus open arguments to further inquiry. (Mills 1959: 34.)

In biology, the differentiation between general and specific aspects of the evolutionary process has not recently been of great concern. Modern evolutionary biology has chosen to confine itself to the phylogenetic course of life; as noted before, the heralded "modern synthetic theory" is wholly devoted to this. The true "triumphant synthesis" which would unify the particular and general facets of evolution does not exist in biology.

Yet failure to distinguish specific and general evolution, it seems to us, has occasioned some confusion in biology about the nature of evolutionary progress. All-round progress is not detached from relative, specific progression, which apparently leads many biologists, even eminent ones such as Simpson, to virtually deny that progress is a general consequence of evolution. In fact, in a recent article Simpson insists that evolution is only "historical" (i.e., specific) and denies that comparative anatomical studies (i.e., general evolution) are evolutionary at all:

In comparative anatomy some such sequence as dogfish-frog-cat-man is still frequently taught as "evolutionary," i.e., historical. In fact the anatomical differences among those organisms are in large part ecologically and behaviorally determined, are divergent and not sequential, and *do not in any useful sense form a historical series.* The same objection applies with perhaps even greater force to studies of behavior which state or assume an evolutionary (historical) sequence in, for instance, comparison of an insect ("invertebrate level"), a rat ("primitive mammalian level"), and a man. (1958: 11; emphasis ours.)

Simpson is not willing to rise above the phylogenetic perspective that dominates biology today. The cultural anthropologist will recognize current biological dogmas such as "all progress is relative"—which is false—and "historically divergent forms defy sequential classification by levels of development." They are precisely the dicta that have held back the study of general cultural evolution for the last sixty years. It is almost as if biologists have fallen before a sterile "cultural analogy."

Julian Huxley should be exempted from this stricture, for he has long insisted on separating the over-all progressive from the divergent trends in evolution. Indeed, Huxley considers the former far more important than diversity, which he characterizes as, "a mere frill of variety . . . a biological luxury, without bearing upon the major and continuing trends of the evolutionary process" (1942: 389). When one considers how much thought, effort, expense, and interest is now vested in biology on a "mere frill of variety," Huxley's assertion is really startling, if not revolutionary. But it is not our intention to begin revolutionary agitations, particularly in what is not our own fatherland.

The traditional evolutionary concerns of anthropology have been precisely the reverse of those in biology, for until recently general evolution rather than specific has occupied first place in evolutionary anthropology. The way the great nineteenth-century cultural evolutionists, Tylor, Spencer, and Morgan, classified and considered cultures indicates that they were principally interested in general progress. Their procedure was to determine *stages* of development and to exemplify them with contemporaneous cultures.

For this reason alone it would be difficult to support the charge that evolutionary theory was grafted wholesale from biology onto culture, or that it was only "biological analogy." It also seems grossly inaccurate, however frequently it is done, to characterize the perspective of the anthropological pioneers as "unilinear," which is the idea that every culture in particular goes through the same general stages. The locus of unilinear evolution-ism is not in anthropology, but, as we have seen with respect to the problem of feudalism, in "crude Marxism" (this phrase is a kind of current redundancy) and Bour-geois History . . . strange bedfellows. Considering only their procedures and obvious objectives—and not what they or others have said *ad hoc* about these—the nine-teenth-century anthropological evolutionists should be acquitted of the unilinear charge, once and for all. Be-cause the specific aspect of evolution was not given much attention does not warrant a criticism which says, in effect, that it was lumped with the general, thus yielding unilinear evolution. The error, if any, was omission not commission. And even so, we recall Spencer's words, "Like other kinds of progress, social progress is *not linear* but divergent and re-divergent" (our emphasis).

But they are dead, and it probably doesn't matter too much if exonerated or not. What progress has evolution-ary anthropology made since the nineteenth century? The current revival of evolutionism in anthropology is, with the exception of White, decisively specifically ori-ented. By and large, it is particularistic and historically oriented, as anthropology in general has been throughout our century. Steward's "multilinear evolution" is now widely accepted and respectable. This is a gain, for as a platform, multilinear evolution conceivably embraces all of the specific trends in cultural evolution. But at what cost shall we secure this gain? In practice, Steward confines his attention to "regularities," which is to say, parallel developments in unrelated cultural lines (e.g., 1949; 1953; 1955), and at the same time belabors any more general evolutionary concerns. If anthropology continues on this theoretical course, then it can only fail to cope with the larger problem of the origin of diversity, not to mention the whole field of general evolution. Thus the total effect of widespread approval of Steward's position will mean undue limitation, a continuation of the reaction against the nineteenth century.

The historical orientation of twentieth-century American anthropology and of much of its current evolutionism has occasioned a rich controversy in recent years about the relation between "history" and "evolution." A set of interconnected issues are involved: (1) Is evolution to be concerned with historical developments in particular cultures or not? (2) Is environment a relevant, variable factor in the explanation of evolution or an irrelevant, constant factor? (3) Is evolution "history," or are these different real processes? The chief antagonists in the controversy are Kroeber (1946), Steward (1953; 1955), and White (1945; 1949; 1959a).

White distinguishes history as unique sequences of events located in time and space, whereas evolution is the progression of forms not considered in reference to specific times and places:

In the evolutionist process we are not concerned with unique events, fixed in time and place, but with a *class* of events without reference to specific times and places . . . The historian—devotes himself to a specific sequence of particular events; the evolutionist, to a sequence of events as a general process of transformation. (1945: 238.)

Since evolution does not deal with specifics, since it is concerned with classes of cultural forms, culture is considered as a whole and particular environments are not relevant, in White's view:

The functioning of any particular culture will of course be conditioned by local environmental conditions. But in a consideration of culture as a whole, we may average all environments together to form a constant factor which may be excluded from our formula of cultural development. (1949: 368.)

Not many accept White's attempt to distinguish history from evolution; many profess not to understand it. Perhaps that is why White is labelled a "neoevolutionary," although, as he says, all he states is the general evolutionary perspective of the nineteenth century.

Kroeber, in an exchange with White, insists that evolution is primarily the historic process, and that historians "do" evolution (1946). Murdock goes Kroeber one better: "The only cultural processes are historical," he writes (1949: 116n). And ten years later, ". . . evolution consists of real events, not of abstractions from events, so that evolutionary development is historical in the strictest and most literal sense" (1959: 129). Likewise, for Steward (multilinear) evolution is concerned with, "significant parallels in culture *history* . . . inevitably concerned with historical reconstruction" (1955: 28, 18; emphasis ours). In turn, parallel development is parallel adaptation to *environment;* environmental considerations are indispensable (Steward 1955).

The distinction between general and specific evolution is relevant to—and we think, resolves—the debate. The historic development of particular cultural forms is specific evolution, phylogenetic transformation through adaptation. Environment, both natural and superorganic, is obviously essential to the understanding of such processes. The progression of *classes* of forms, or in other words, the succession of culture through stages of overall progress, is general evolution. This process is neither phylogenetic nor as such adaptive; consequently, environment is "constant," or better, irrelevant. That process which Kroeber labels "history," Steward, "multilinear

43

evolution," and Murdock, "evolution," is the specific aspect of the grand evolutionary movement; that which White names "evolution" is the general aspect. Adopting the grand-movement perspective suggested here, evolution is in one respect "history," but in another not; in one aspect it involves particular events, but in another classes thereof; in one respect environment is relevant, but in another it is to be excluded from consideration. Each of the participants in the controversy is in one respect "right" but in another "wrong"—from our standpoint.

And, if we may be permitted to press home the implications, it seems to us then that evolutionism is the central, inclusive, organizing outlook of anthropology, comparable in its theoretical power to evolutionism in biology. ". . . the great principle that every scholar must lay firm hold of . . ."

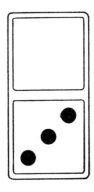

Adaptation and Stability

Adaptation, the securing and conserving of control over environment, is the orienting process of the specific evolution of both life and culture. And in both the biological and the superorganic realm, the adaptive process has two characteristic aspects: creative and conservative. On the one hand there is the evolution of specialized structures and patterns that enable a culture or a population of organisms to achieve a requisite measure of adjustment to its environmental setting. On the other hand there is a tendency toward stabilization, the conservation of the adaptive structures and modes that have been achieved.

THE MECHANICS OF CULTURAL ADAPTATION

Having chosen to focus this essay on adaptation, particularly cultural adaptation, we have prejudged its perspective on the mechanics of cultural development. In Chapter II, it has been pointed out that different taxonomic outlooks are required for the study of general as opposed to specific evolution. Here it is suggested in addition that the view one adopts regarding the relation between parts and subsystems of a culture and regarding the generative causes of development also differs according to the type of evolutionary change, adaptive or progressive, under investigation. The kind of explanation

45

appropriate for general progress is not appropriate for specific adaptation.

Leslie White's perception of cultural organization may be taken to exemplify the explanatory perspective of general evolutionism. A culture, in this view, consists of three interrelated subsystems, technological, sociological, and ideological. The technological component is the fundamental determinant of the others and technological development is the impetus for general progress.

We may view a cultural system as a series of three horizontal strata: the technological layer on the bottom, the philosophical on the top, the sociological stratum in between. These positions express their respective roles in the culture process. The technological system is basic and primary. Social systems are functions of technologies; and philosophies express technological forces and reflect social systems. The technological factor is therefore *the* determinant of a cultural system as a whole . . . This is not to say, of course, that social systems do not condition the operation of technologies, or that social and technological systems are not affected by philosophies. They do and are. But to condition is one thing; to determine, quite another. (1949: 366.)

It is important to observe that White here views culture as a *closed system*. That is, culture is taken out of particular and historic contexts. Considered *as such*, White is saying, without regard to the actual course of development or environmental circumstances, the general form of the social and (more or less directly) the ideological spheres of a culture is determined by its technological attainment. It certainly is valid and fruitful to consider culture as a closed system and technology as the impetus of progress if one's concern is general evolution. But when attention shifts to adaptation, to specific evolution, then culture is properly considered as an *open system* and the mechanics of its development are differently understood.

In specific historical-environmental circumstances culture is an open system entering into relation with nature and with other cultures. The character of its habitat will influence a culture's technology, and through technology its social and ideological components. But nearby cultures and the relations effected with them also affect a culture's sociopolitical and ideological subsystems. Moreover, the latter may in turn, in the attempt to cope with the outside world, channel the direction of technological development. To take a current example: the reason that America is presently expending great labors in the production of guided missiles is not a *sui generis* function of her technology. Rather, the reason lies in America's political relation to other world powers. The fact is that America's sociopolitical organization, in significant part shaped by international conditions, is directly influencing her course of technological growth. It may be cogently argued that America acts in given ways politically only out of economic necessity. But this does not deny that the American polity has been in good measure structured by external circumstances and that it is determining how nature's resources are to be employed and to what ends. While it is true that the technological result will set America's general level of evolutionary standing and even influence the organization of society itself, it is equally true that society, especially its political aspect, will have determined the general degree as well as the specific form of technological achievement.

The specific perspective on evolution involves a conception of culture as an open or adaptive system. Adaptation embraces both relation to nature and, except for completely isolated societies, to other cultural systems.

Evolution and Culture

Adaptation to nature will shape a culture's technology and derivatively its social and ideological components. Yet adaptation to other cultures may shape society and ideology which in turn act upon technology and determine its further course. The total result of the adaptive process is the production of an organized cultural whole, an integrated technology, society, and ideology, which copes with the dual selective influences of nature on the one hand and the impact of outside cultures on the other. Such are, in general outline, the mechanics of cultural adaptation.

It may be parenthetically remarked that failure to make the distinction between culture as a closed system, the view of general evolution, and culture as an open system, the outlook of specific evolution, may have been a cause for the premature rejection of White's philosophy of culture among other anthropologists. Dealing with specific cases, the experiences of ethnographers regarding the causes of cultural development are extremely varied. One may see a village "choose progress" upon exposure to an alien ideology, a philosophical change that is then followed by important social and economic *consequences*. Has not the Christian religion, if not the Protestant Ethic, affected social and economic practice among many primitive peoples the world over? An Asiatic society may undergo a revolution stimulated by intellectuals agitating with slogans of a German philosopher, only later consolidating politically as a nation, and still later, if ever, developing the industry that can support its ideological and political status. Having examined numerous cases of radical cultural innovation that are not locally technologically caused, anthropologists are wont to reject the "materialist" conception of evolution out of hand. The point is that White's view, relevant to the explanation of general progress, does not specify the causes of adaptive change in particular cases.

We have in passing necessarily commented on the dual nature of a culture's environment, the fact that both habitat and other cultures comprise selective influences. This deserves some explication if only because it is frequently neglected in studies of "cultural ecology," which tend to ignore, at some peril, intercultural relations. When we look at nations, whose relations with other nations are often decisive for survival, it is obvious that at least part of an adaptive explanation of the prevailing forms of polity, ideology and other aspects of culture must lie in the matter of intercultural adjustment. Yet this is equally so for less-developed cultures. One might point, for example, to Barth's recent demonstration of the development and perpetuation of cultural differences by ethnic segmentation and economic interdependence among the Pathans, Kohistani, and Gujars of North Pakistan (1956). Significantly, Barth finds a "natural area" approach inadequate, and uses instead the idea of ecologic niche as "the place of a group in the *total* environment, its relation to resources *and* competitors" (*ibid.*: 1079; emphasis ours).

Without consideration of the cultural aspect of an ecologic niche, evolutionary anthropology is unnecessarily prevented from viewing diffusion and acculturation in a developmental context; hence, that pervasive process of specific cultural evolution, convergence by coalescence, escapes us if the superorganic environment is ignored. The necessity of this wider view of environment for an understanding of cultural adaptation is a continuing emphasis of this chapter. "Cultural ecology" simply must embrace the relations between cultures, the superorganic setting, as well as the natural features of habitat, just as "ecology" in biological studies includes the organic environment, competing species, as well as the inorganic.

SOME CONSEQUENCES OF ADAPTATION

One of the major consequences of adaptation for culture as a whole has been the production of cultures in particular, the production of diversity. In Spencer's words, "there have arisen genera and species of societies." Indeed, Darwin's "principle of divergence," that the greatest amount of life can be supported by greatest diversification of structure, may be applied as suitably to culture. It is the structural diversification of man's extra-somatic means of survival and adjustment that has permitted the continued increase of man himself at the expense of other forms of life. Culture, differentiating into *cultures* by adaptation, has made possible the exploitation of the great variety of the earth's resources.

Probably the most common condition in which cultural divergence or speciation occurs is the juxtaposition of societies and their competition within a varied environment. In the process of adaptation, different societies will become technologically and in other ways specialized for the exploitation of particular facets of the environment. Culture, so to speak, divides its labor of exploiting nature among different societies, and variations in culture ensue in consequence. A number of examples—including Barth's study mentioned above—come readily to mind, such as the development of mixed farming, pastoral, and transhumant modes of existence along the borders of the Asiatic steppe, or the differentiation of riverine, agricultural, and pastoral cultures in West Africa.

Another common condition for cultural divergence is the presence of an open and diverse habitat into which a culture can expand. Expansion into a large, diversified area gives rise to the process of extensive variation known in evolutionary biology as *adaptive radiation*, ecological divergence on a grand scale. The adaptive radiation of life forms involves the outward spread of a generalized group followed by progressive differentiation of species by adaptive modification in which the various populations become more efficient with respect to particular modes of life (Huxley 1943: 487). Sahlins (1958) has suggested the appropriateness of the concept of adaptive radiation for the differentiation of social systems by adaptation in Polynesia, and possibly the study of other ethnographic provinces would profit from this approach. A further illustration of the applicability of the concept for cultural evolution is to be found in V. Gordon Childe's discussion of the early spread and diversification of neolithic culture in Europe—one phase of what may be termed the Neolithic Radiation. By the beginning of the 4th millennium B.C., much of Europe was occupied by four distinctive and widely spread cultures, each of which displayed great uniformity throughout its area of occupation (Childe 1958: 44). Following the early period of neolithic colonization, each of the four spread into new habitats and there was a breaking up into regional cultural variants by adaptation to particular local conditions.

The early phase of the neolithic radiation in Europe presents trends of increasing efficiency through adaptive specialization. This is particularly apparent in Childe's description of the spread and regional development of the best known of the four primary cultures, the Danubian (1958; 1951). Movement into and adaptation to particular environments in culture, as in life, however, sometimes result in *simplification*, the sacrifice of specialized parts that are vital in other environments. Albert G.

Keller focused on this type of adaptation in his evolutionary approach to the study of colonization. The pioneer culture of seventeenth- and eighteenth-century America represents a simplification of a protoindustrial, commercial culture to the level of Iron Age technology (with the exception of firearms) and the self-sufficiency of household economy, in which production is for use and relatively simple patterns of exchange, reciprocity, and cooperative enterprise prevail. The Yankee "jack-of-all-trades" reflects strikingly the self-sufficiency characteristic of frontier culture.

Yet more than that, the loss of specialized parts involved in the frontier adaptation left a generalized culture that was highly efficient in dealing with an extensive, relatively open environment. Interesting in this connection is the interpretation, popular in historical circles, that traces the superior achievements of American civilization to its frontier origins. A break with the cumbersome preindustrial traditions of Europe—the "Slaying of the European Father" as one historian has phrased it—allowed a rapid and unimpeded evolution from an initial rudimentary level. This interpretation partly expresses a significant evolutionary principle, namely, the developmental advantages of relatively nonspecialized culture types when presented with an opportunity such as a rich and open environment. (The subject of the evolutionary potential of generalized types is pursued further in Chapter V.)

Cultural parasitism and the formation of "part-cultures" also fall within this class of adaptive phenomena, though in these cases simplification results in a loss of self-sufficiency. Kroeber pointed out that "Degeneration or simplification is a factor in cultural as well as natural history. . . . Even the suppression of parts due to parasitism has its cultural parallels: quite probably among the Negritos and among pastoral nomads in contact with farming and town populations" (1952: 60). One may wonder at first glance what warrants the inclusion of cultural "degeneration" or simplification in a discussion devoted to creative adaptation. It is not the stabilization that is the usual consequence of simplification, as in the examples offered by Kroeber, but the great creative potential which can also result from such processes—exemplified by colonial America—that is of special interest here.

Divergence through specialization, adaptive radiation, simplification, and the like is not the only consequence of cultural adaptation. There is also convergence through parallel adaptation and through cultural coalescence or acculturation. Both of these forms of convergence are so thoroughly familiar that we need not dwell upon them. Our discussion of adaptation in general has perhaps been sufficient to indicate how the study of cultural innovation and transmission as carried on by anthropologists, historians, and other specialists may profitably be viewed, or better reviewed, in the evolutionary context. We turn now to a less understood and much neglected aspect of adaptation, cultural stability or conservation.

CULTURAL STABILITY

A culture is an integrated organization of technology, social structure, and philosophy adjusted to the life problems posed by its natural habitat and by nearby and often competing cultures. The process of adjustment or adaptation, however, inevitably involves specialization, a one-sided development that tends to preclude the possibility of change in other directions, to impede adaptive response to changed environmental conditions. While adaptation is creative, then, it is also self-limiting. A particular technology requires particular social adaptations for wielding it, and conversely a given social order is perpetuated by co-ordinated deployment of technology. Thus, whereas a given technological development may generate a new organization of society, the latter in turn operates to preserve the technology that gave rise to it. Metal implements fashioned by techniques designed for stone materials, a movement of handicraftsmen which involves the destruction of newly developed textile machinery, the purchase of patent rights by corporations to prevent their being used—these illustrate the role of social systems in resisting or actively inhibiting changes that would disrupt or modify the existing culture (White 1959: 27). Ideological systems, too, are inherently conservative and backward-looking, deriving their authority and sanction from conditions of the past. The ideals and values of most cultures take continuance and changelessness for granted.

That cultures tend to maintain a status quo is not only deducible by logical conjecture on the nature of culture and its subsystems. The tendency toward stability is, empirically speaking, thoroughly familiar to anthropologists. The historic, archaeological, and ethnographic records attest to numerous instances of the persistence, "survival," or "inertia," of cultural traditions, particular cultures, and elements or traits. Indeed, one might formulate it as a general principle, The Principle of Stabilization, that a culture at rest tends to remain at rest.

A corollary of the principle of stabilization may also be pointed out. When acted upon by external forces a culture will, if necessary, undergo specific changes only to the extent of and with the effect of *preserving* unchanged its fundamental structure and character. Robert

Adaptation and Stability

Braidwood appreciated this principle in a description of the Paleolithic cultures of Europe at the end of the Pleistocene. He writes:

The upsets that came with the melting of the last glaciers caused all sorts of changes in tools and in food-getting habits, but the people of Europe in 5,000 B.C. or even later were still just as much simple hunters, fishers, and food collectors as they had been in 25,000 B.C. . . . In other words, they changed just enough so that they would not have to change. . . . (1948: 79–80.)

An example of more restricted scope is provided by the Yakut of northeastern Siberia. Formerly inhabitants of Central Asia, the Yakut were separated from other Turkic tribes by the Mongol invasions of the thirteenth century. Later they were forced northward into the Lena River Valley by the Mongol Buryats, and with Russian penetration of the Lena region in the seventeenth century Yakut groups moved farther northeastward and occupied the Yana, Indighirka, and Kolyma valleys. In spite of the severity of their new tundra habitat, many Yakut remained "typical representatives of the culture of the nomadic or seminomadic horse and cattle-breeding Turkic tribes of Central Asia" (Jochelson 1933: 197).

Interest in the horse pervaded all major sectors of Yakut culture. In the single-minded concern for their animals that is typical of pastoralists, the horse was "almost worshipped." The Yakut were, therefore, little interested in the reindeer breeding of their neighbors, such as the Tungus, and in the southern part of their territory where agriculture was practicable, its adoption was resisted until 1853. It was not without suffering, however, that Yakut culture was maintained in this inimical environment. Jochelson describes the difficulties and hardships of the

Yakut in sustaining their herds during the long winters. For two-thirds of the year the animals were stalled in earth huts. The quantities of hay required were enormous, and the summers were actively spent in haymaking, to the partial neglect of the productive activities of fishing. Still, as Jochelson reports, often only 50% of the required hay was procured and much of this was of poor quality (*ibid.:* 188). It is little wonder that the animals were "always hungry" and famine frequent among their providers.

In addition to the changes already indicated, the Yakut were forced to adopt earth huts in place of tents, to acquire reindeer and dogs, and to attempt to compensate for the meager food supply of their horses by feeding them meat and fish (they also attempted unsuccessfully to feed hay to their reindeer). They were even forced to saddle and ride cows in place of horses that had died or become too weakened by the deficient diet and the severe climate (Forde 1957: 400; Jochelson 1905–8, II: 480). Additional modifications that could be listed would only further support the observation that the Yakut, too, "changed just enough so that they would not have to change."

It may still seem paradoxical to the reader that adaptive modifications produce stability, that there is change and yet there is no change. The discussion of some additional, important features of stability, introduced by way of analogy, will aid in this context. In the study of demography, populations are described as having structures defined by various criteria, such as proportions of age groups. While a given population may vary through time in absolute numbers, it is considered stable as long as its structure is maintained. Similarly, cultures are structured by their adaptive orientations and requirements.

Because of new exigencies, specific changes may be re·
quired to maintain the structure, and in addition, traits
that are relatively "free" from selective pressures of adaptation may enter or leave the system with no consequent
alteration of structure. We must warn, however, that
one cannot tell beforehand what traits may or may not
come to play adaptive roles in stabilization. No class or
classes of cultural elements are inherently more suited for
adaptive functions than others. It depends upon the environmental factors present, as well as on the resources
a particular culture has at hand or can borrow from outside. Thus, carved statuary in an intensified and modified
form, assumed important adaptive functions in maintaining Polynesian ramage organization in the unusual environment of Easter Island (Sahlins 1955; see Chapter
II). Among the Iroquois the elaboration and sanctification
of the mnemonic and symbolic functions of wampum
served to maintain confederacy organization (Harding
1959). Note that these and other examples the reader
might supply for himself represent creative adaptations,
innovative alterations or additions to a culture. But at
the same time, because of their functions in stabilization,
such features have a conservative, antiprogressive character in the sense of *general progress*.

It must also be remembered that stabilization is a process
in itself, induced and necessitated by environmental
(natural or superorganic) factors, and that the tempo as
well as the success of the process is determined by the
rate and character of environmental modifications. It may
happen, for example, that the alteration of some aspect
of environment is so sudden and devastating that no new
equilibrium state is possible. In such a case, cultural
(though not necessarily human) extinction could be the
result. Or it may happen that during periods of rapid

change, or when environmental changes are of such a quantity, rate, and character that whole series of internally and externally directed adjustments are set off, the equilibrium point itself is set in motion. However, this latter possibility should not be allowed to obscure what is really significant—the persistent tendency toward stability that is characteristic of all cultural systems.

Further exemplification of the mechanisms of stabilization will be offered in subsequent paragraphs, but first attention must be directed to a controversy that is made explicit by the formulation of stabilization as a general principle.

The principle of cultural stabilization is in opposition to, but is not belied by, the pervasive assumption in contemporary anthropological thinking that "cultures are continually changing." For example, Linton prefaces a discussion of processes of culture change with the statement that "All cultures, even the simplest, seem to be in a continuous state of change" (1955: 41; cf. also Gillin 1948: 524, 533; Sorokin 1957: Chapter 38; Turney-High 1949: 66–67), and Herskovits introduces a similar discussion with the following:

A society may be never so small, never so isolated; its technological equipment may be of the simplest, its devotion to its own way of life expressed in extreme conservatism; yet changes constantly take place as generation succeeds generation, and new ideas, new alignments, new techniques come into the thinking of its members. For no living culture is static. (1945: 143.)

Both Linton and Herskovits have utilized this principle in criticizing the approaches of nineteenth-century evolution. The characteristic stability of primitive societies was strongly expressed by early evolutionists, such as Spencer and Maine, and also in Tylor's theory of survivals. The idea that cultures could become arrested in development enabled the reconstruction of evolutionary events from contemporary ethnographic data and increased the range and effectiveness of the comparative method. However, Linton and Herskovits argue that the universality of culture change disproves the assumption of the early evolutionists that primitive cultures can be regarded as "examples of development arrested at various stages." "The technique of equating living 'primitive' peoples with early man has been found methodologically inacceptable, given the known propensity of all cultures to change" (Herskovits 1948: 630).

It is interesting that Linton, who considered cultural arrestment merely "wishful thinking" on the part of certain early evolutionists, also stated that primitive cultures "represent the terminal points of divergent lines of cultural development. The one point at which certain of the 'primitive' cultures of today can be said to resemble early stages in the development of our own is in their *technology and its social consequences*" (1955: 49; our emphasis). Needless to say, this "one point" of resemblance is an extremely broad and crucial one, and seems to us at least, to confirm cultural arrestment as a valid assumption.

The principle of stabilization as considered here, however, is more than a convenient methodological device for exploring the prehistoric past; it is a statement about the nature of culture, and becomes in itself a very significant phenomenon for study. It means that cultures tend to persist unchanged, and under the influence of external factors act to maintain their basic structure through adaptive modification. Yet it would seem that for at least some anthropologists there are semantic and methodological objections to the concept of cultural stability or equilibrium. Gillin states that the term "equilibrium" ". . . seems to suffer from the semantic difficulty that . . . it implies a condition of rest, complete static stability. Since no cultural system is ever completely static, we need a concept and vocabulary which can also be applied to dynamic conditions of a system" (1948: 524). Chemists, economists, sociologists (including the British social anthropologists), biologists and other scientists, however, have utilized the concept of equilibrium without losing sight of the dynamic character of their phenomena. One wonders why this should constitute a special difficulty for anthropologists.

Herskovits raises objections of a different sort. The problem of stability is difficult to study, he says, because it is "couched in negative terms." (He conceives stability negatively, i.e., as resistance to change, 1948: 485–88.) Furthermore, it is only on rare occasions that an ethnographer would be able to "witness the force of conservatism at work" in the society he is studying. Even when we ask why so little change has occurred among such conservative groups as the Eskimo and aboriginal Australians, continues Herskovits, "we are reduced to speculation" (see, however, the discussion of the Eskimo in Chapter IV). It would appear also that for Herskovits stability has the unfavorable connotation of "stagnation," implying particularly that primitives lack capacity for advancement, which is seen to be in opposition to the axiom of cultural relativism.

Apparently such difficulties have not been recognized or been as serious for others. Boas, Kroeber, and Lowie, to mention but a few, have appreciated stability as a characteristic and important feature of cultural systems, and have offered explanations of it. Still, within American anthropology there has been no explicit formulation of stabilization as a general principle, nor adequate examination of its bases and consequences in cultural terms. Both stability and change have been persistently treated as psychological questions and accordingly both have been "explained" in psychological—not to mention anthropomorphic—terms (see Boas 1928: Chapter VII; Lowie 1940: 377–81). The problem of cultural stability is reduced to that of individual conformity, while change is seen to consist of variations in individual behavior. Conformity may then be explained, of course, in terms of education, enculturation, habit, authority, "devotion to the *status quo*," and the like. A host of factors can be arrayed to account for behavioral variation: the "wish for new experience," the "play instinct," man's "itch to tinker with his environment," and so *ad infinitum*. (Whether a culture is stable or changing, then, depends on the relative strength of the contending forces, habits or wishes, education or itches!) The supposed "continuous change" of all cultures is interpreted similarly:

The constant revision and expansion of his [man's] social heredity is a result of some inner drive, not of outer necessity. It seems that man enjoys playing with both his mind and his muscles. The skilled craftsman is not content with endless repetitions. He takes delight in setting and solving for himself new problems of creation. The thinker derives pleasure from speculating about all sorts of things which are of no practical importance, while the individuals who lack the ability to create with either hand or mind are alert to learn new things. It seems probable that the human capacity for being bored, rather than man's social or natural needs, lies at the root of man's cultural advance. (Linton 1936: 90.)

On a number of occasions White (e.g., 1949) has decisively exposed the fallacies and sterility of such psychologistic and indeterministic interpretations for the scientific study of culture, and no further criticism will be undertaken here. It is a matter of great significance, however, in noting the opposition of "stability" and "continuous change," that they proceed from and form parts of totally different concepts of culture and its study. Cultural arrestment and stabilization were assumptions of nineteenth-century evolutionism, and are confirmed as important generalizations by the empirical findings of present evolutionary research. Underlying the principle of stabilization are 1) the concept of cultures as thermodynamic systems which may be analyzed in terms of the relations of their technoeconomic, sociologic, and philosophic subsystems, and 2) an interpretative approach combining the methods of culturology and ecology. The principle of continuous change, on the other hand, has found its home largely within the particularistic and psychologically oriented American tradition of ethnology of the present century. Cultures are conceived in atomistic or in psychological terms, as assemblages of variously (only) historically related traits and complexes, or the sum total of individual behavior of the group, depending on which of the two dominant approaches are employed: historical-diffusionist or psychological. The fundamental importance of the principle of continuous change for the historical perspective is expressed by Herskovits (1945: 146): "The essential historical approach to the study of living non-literate folk is based on the assumption that culture is dynamic, and thus in process of continuous change."

The reader may already have objected that nothing more is signified by "continuous change" than the simple philosophic notion of Heraclitus and the other pre-Socratic philosophers that the universe and all things composing it are in eternal flux. If this were the case, then there would scarcely be need or basis for rejecting the notion. The question arises, though, why such an obvious principle—quite irrelevant for the understanding of cultural change—is stated so frequently, while less obvious assumptions remain only implicit and more important ones, such as stability, are neglected. Furthermore, if pre-Socratic thought is to be a source for cultural principles, then anthropologists might benefit by greater thoroughness of research:

Heraclitus . . . probably expressed the universality of change more clearly than his predecessors; but for him it was the obverse idea of the *measure* inhering in change, the stability that persists through it, that was of vital importance. (Kirk and Raven 1957: 187.)

The principle that all cultures are characterized by continuous change definitely has deeper significance. This is evidenced by its widespread and repeated expression in a variety of contexts and its extensive documentation: its use as an antievolutionist device and as a kind of support for extreme cultural relativism; its statement as an assumption of the "essential historical approach" to primitive societies; and its links with certain sterile propositions about the nature of cultural phenomena. It is in these distorted proportions that the principle of continuous change, and its varied implications, are antithetical to the view of cultures as directively organized adaptive systems, and to the evolutionary perspective as a whole.

To return to our discussion of stability, examples of the conservative functions of modification in relation to changes in the natural environment have already been offered. It is equally characteristic that cultures undergo changes, in response to the influence of superorganic environment, that are nonprogressive and specifically designed to resist reorganization, that actually foster stability and continuity. Generally speaking, in the interaction of cultures the types of adaptive mechanisms that are so employed depend on 1) the kind of intercultural relationship, and 2) the level of development of the respective cultures. For example, a culture defending itself from another more or less equally advanced culture could normally be expected to compete technologically and sociopolitically in warfare. On the other hand, in the relations of dominant with decidedly "weaker" cultures lacking effective technology and social organization for war, ideology becomes the main means of defense. This is illustrated by the widespread phenomenon of nativistic movements or cults, in which a supernaturalistic philosophy is developed and utilized in organizing a social movement of resistance to the encroachments of a dominant, more powerful culture.

We conclude by offering two detailed examples of the tendency toward stabilization in the face of selective pressures emanating from the superorganic environment. The first is the formation of closed corporate communities as described by Eric Wolf, and the second the modifications occurring in the potlatch system of the Northwest Coast as it was adjusted to the conditions of the nineteenth-century Euroamerican market.

The corporate peasant community is a specialized local structure that is capable of instituting stable relationships with a dominant, enveloping cultural system. The corporate community is the offspring, says Wolf, ". . . of the dualization of society into a dominant entrepreneurial sector and a dominated sector of native peasants" (1957: 8). A clearly demarcated sociocultural system, territorially based and self-governing, the closed corporate community is the means by which the dominated peasant sector staves off the penetration of entrepreneurial culture; it is a means of cultural self-defense. Economic autonomy is the bastion of the corporate peasantry. Land is either held communally or in private holdings with strict prohibition of sale to outsiders. Production continues to be production for use within the community, despite the orientation of production for exchange that characterizes the larger society. Surpluses that may result from familial differences in agricultural production or from outside sources are siphoned off by sponsoring village ceremonies or by other forms of redistribution. In this way the community as a whole remains on an economic dead level, and the formation of the *kulak* and other entrepreneurial social relations are decidedly inhibited. The ideology of the community joins its economic system in preserving the *status quo*. Corporate villages are philosophically characterized by what Wolf has called "localocentric attitudes" and also by a "cult of poverty" in which greed is denounced and "resignation in the face of poverty is accorded high value" (1957: 5). Moreover, "institutionalized envy," gossip and witchcraft directed against those who assume the material trappings or the attitude of "upward climbing" of the outer world, operate to maintain economic equality and traditional behavior.

Turning to the Northwest Coast potlatch, there appear to be four factors that are most significant for understanding the changes that the potlatch system underwent: 1) the influx of European trade goods, 2) individual economic opportunities that were presented to the Indians, 3) resettlement of populations around trading posts, and 4) the decimation of native populations through disease. The potlatch system was highly successful in adjusting to these conditions. In the face of encroaching capitalist culture it became the main instrument for preserving a way of life which maintained great disparity in social status for the sake of equality in wealth.

European trade goods, and later cash incomes from employment in canneries, the lumbering industry, and other occupations, resulted in the gradual expansion of potlatching until in the latter nineteenth-century thousands of the woolen trade blankets were distributed annually. Individual economic opportunities led to the development of individualistic patterns in which the potlatch became an occasion for personal glorification rather than for stressing the importance of the lineage (Colson 1953: 81). The competitive potlatch, which contrasts with the spirit of generosity, gratitude, and good will characteristic of potlatching in early times (Barnett 1938), developed among Kwakiutl and Tsimshian groups that assembled at trading posts and formed loose confederations. Since it was inevitable that the various groups of the confederations would potlatch, and since potlatch gifts were distributed in order of rank, there had to be a way of ranking the various chiefs intertribally. As Drucker explains, they ". . . were faced with the knotty problem of integrating their respective series of ranked chiefs into a single order of precedence" (1951: 456–57). Competition, vengeance, and rivalrous destruction of property became the means to this end. In addition, the rapid decrease in native populations meant that chiefs died without proper heirs, and that potlatch positions, names and lineage crests were quite out of proportion to the population (Codere 1950; Drucker 1955: 122). As a consequence people of low rank were able to enter the potlatch system.

The potlatch was adaptively modified in a number of

specific ways: 1) expansion in terms of the amount of goods distributed; 2) the development of individualistic and competitive patterns; and 3) the participation of low status individuals, who, perhaps with an extra measure of enthusiasm for the social rewards of prestige, strove to perpetuate the system. Yet these modifications combined to preserve the fundamental, old-time economic function of the potlatch and the social relations associated with that function. The potlatch continued to be the means of equidistribution of goods among individuals and groups with variable access to wealth, the sacrifice of goods being compensated by prestige. Into late post-contact times, as Drucker stated, the effect of the potlatch ". . . was to periodically assemble and redistribute blankets and cash" (1951: 385). Radin called the tribes of the Northwest Coast "the capitalists of the North." But when it is considered that blankets were virtually the currency of trade, then the potlatch must be understood as precisely designed to *prevent* the formation of capitalist relations, for the periodic dispersal of blankets totally prevented "primitive accumulation."

The purpose of this chapter has been to define the role and significance of adaptation for the evolutionary perspective. The discussion has in some measure, it is hoped, clarified the nature and relatedness of various phenomena of acculturation, ecology, peasant societies, and archaeology in the light of this perspective. Initially, two sectors of environment were distinguished, natural and superorganic, and the importance of the latter for understanding both the creative and conservative aspects of adaptation has been emphasized throughout. Certainly as cultures have gained in expansive power through greater utilization of available energy and evolved with complex social organization and ideologies, so have super-organic factors, through diffusion, become increasingly important in determining specific evolutionary developments. Our topic has been organized in terms of the two characteristic aspects of cultural adaptation, creative and conservative. Through divergence and radiation, convergence and parallel development, new forms and elements of culture are produced. But because of their systemic nature cultures tend toward stability and self-maintenance, and under the influence of external pressures frequently develop special features only for preserving their basic structures and orientations.

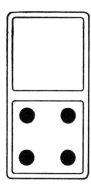

The Law of Cultural Dominance

In the organic world general evolutionary advance is reflected in a succession of what paleontologists call "dominant types," each of which embodies some new structural-functional improvement in its organization. Although many biologists eschew the use of such terms as "progress" or "higher" and "lower" in their studies on the grounds that they rest upon nonscientific value judgments, there appears to be agreement among them as to which were the dominant types in the course of organic evolution. Probably the reason for this agreement is that the empirical measure of dominance—increased adaptability to environmental variety—is readily discerned, not only among living populations but in the fossil record as well.

We believe that there are other, equally objective reasons for speaking in terms of progress and of higher and lower forms; we are not introducing the concept of dominance for this purpose alone. Dominance is a significant characteristic of the evolutionary process and deserves elaboration in its own right for the uses it has. But here, as in previous chapters, we must diverge somewhat from the standardized use of certain conceptions of the characteristics of evolution. Just as we have distinguished specific evolution from general evolution, so we should

69

speak of two different perspectives on dominance. These we shall also label specific and general.

Because specific evolution involves adaptive specialization, the dominance achieved in this process is always bounded by the borders of the environment to which the species is adjusting. This environment does not become wider during the process of specialization; if anything, it frequently becomes an ever-narrowing "niche." The dominance over competing species in that environment becomes more and more complete, with the result that upon ultimate success the victorious species is finally the sole exploiter of the contested resources of its niche.

If specific evolution leads to increasing *adaptation*, it can be said that general evolution leads to greater *adaptability*—which is not the same thing. In one important respect general dominance has an attribute contrary to specific dominance. A higher, more progressive type in the general evolutionary sense has adaptability which *extends* the ecological horizon. Instead of digging a deeper and deeper environmental groove for itself the advanced species spreads laterally to more kinds of environments. (Note that this does not mean that it is "freer" of environment, as is sometimes said.) The specifically dominant and the generally dominant forms are, of course, often in conflict and, as we shall see, it is the form most specifically adapted which has the best chance of maintaining itself in the face of the widening dominance of the higher form. At any rate, there are in the life struggle as in other kinds of competition (such as in the field of scholarship) two kinds of success: greater achievement in a narrowing field and achievement measured by its relative extension or generality.

A new type representing general evolutionary improvement extends its range of dominance on the evolutionary stage by the process of adaptive radiation or multiple specialization, permitting it to exploit a greater environmental variety. The reptiles and later the mammals, for instance, both diversified into carnivores and herbivores, dwarfs and giants, runners and burrowers, fliers and fishlike secondary aquatics. The mammals, however, represented a more progressive step in evolution and were able to supplant the reptiles as the dominant land group because they embodied improvements in temperature regulation, prenatal protection of the young, and a number of other features, all of which made it possible for them to function effectively under a much wider range of environmental conditions than the reptiles ever could.

The various lineages of the form exhibiting general dominance may continue to improve in the specific sense by adapting and becoming more efficient with respect to their own particular ecological setting until their potentialities for further adjustment reach a limit and they become stabilized. Indeed, stabilization seems to have been the fate of most evolutionary trends when they have not suffered the more severe evolutionary fate of total extinction.

Once a form has achieved general dominance by virtue of some new biological invention leading toward greater all-round adaptability, every rival type is cut off from taking a similar evolutionary step unless it does so more efficiently, thereby enabling it to compete successfully with its predecessor. However, if still another form evolves that possesses some improvement enabling a more effective exploitation of the environmental resources, then it will become widely dominant and its success will be established by a rapid and varied deployment accompanied by a victory over and perhaps even total extermination of the previous types. Of course the variety of ecological niches and the modes of filling them are so multitudinous that it is hardly likely that the rise and spread of a new type could possibly extinguish all other types at the lower levels. Mammals could no more fill the environment occupied by beetles than beetles could take the place of amoebas. Moreover, some lineages become so highly specialized and well-adapted to a particular kind of habitat that they are able to maintain a dominance in this environment and hold their own against incursions by later, generally dominant forms. It is not surprising, then, that higher and lower organisms, the "defeated" and the "conquerors," should continue to exist, apparently side by side, inasmuch as the lower may remain specifically dominant in their own niche.

If we briefly survey the facts concerning groups that once held a position of general dominance, we find that some have become totally extinct like the trilobites. Others survive in much reduced form with many of their lineages extinguished as the reptiles, or with their numbers greatly diminished as the large nonhuman placentals. Those which have not suffered reduction of one sort or another have remained virtually unchanged for varying lengths of geologic time, as the insects which have shown no improvement for more than thirty million years or the birds which have changed very little for about twenty million years. (For a detailed discussion of the rise and fall of dominant types, see Wells, Huxley, and Wells 1934: Book I.)

To sum up, the defining characteristics of a general dominant type in the evolution of the organic world are simple and pragmatic. Because of its greater thermodynamic versatility in exploiting varied environments, it is distributed over a wider range than nondominant types. The specific dominant types, on the other hand, have characteristically maintained a monopoly over a narrow range by increased specialization.

DOMINANCE IN CULTURAL EVOLUTION

The course of cultural evolution has similarly been marked by a succession of types each of which has embodied more varied and effective energy-capturing devices and consequently has tended to spread at the expense of its less fortunately endowed predecessors. Since the varieties of ecological niches that cultural systems can fill are far fewer than the almost limitless varieties that can be filled by biological systems, the rise and spread of a new generally dominant culture type is even more dramatic than its biological counterpart. The revolutionary nature and world-wide repercussions of such events as the rise and spread of the agriculturally based Neolithic, the later appearance of state forms and urbanism, and the more recent rise to general dominance of industrially based Western Culture have been recognized by all anthropologists, even those who maintain a nonevolutionary perspective.

Each successive higher culture type has tended to spread farther and faster than previous types until in our own day we find that Western Culture is not only extending its dominance over much of this planet but is also attempting to extend it into outer space as well. The greater potential range of more advanced types has far-reaching implications for the evolutionary process as a whole. Together with the fact that culture is transmitted in space as well as time by nongenetic mechanisms, it accounts for the trend in cultural evolution which is almost totally absent in biological evolution: the trend toward a greater convergence and consequent homogeneity of culture type, accompanied by a decrease in the diversity

73

of cultures. At first glance, this might seem to contradict the often noted trend toward heterogeneity in the evolution of culture. The contradiction, however, is more apparent than real. Certainly it is true that each successive culture type exhibiting general dominance has become increasingly heterogeneous; it is organizationally more complex, with more parts and subparts, and with a greater functional differentiation between them. At the same time the potential range of dominance of each successive culture type has been correspondingly increased. In its spread, the higher type has been able to dominate and reduce the variety of cultural systems by transforming them into copies, more or less exact, of itself. Thus, cultural evolution has moved simultaneously in two directions: on the one hand there is an increasing heterogeneity of the higher cultural type; and on the other hand there is an increasing homogeneity of culture as the diversity of culture types is reduced. Undoubtedly this latter trend toward the homogenization of the world of cultures will continue in the future at a more accelerated rate than in the past.

Since generally advanced types are thermodynamically more versatile and effective in a greater variety of environments, they are able to drive out less advanced types. The great reduction through recent millennia of the hunting and gathering societies of the world is a good case in point. Once the sole occupants of the cultural scene, they have tended to recede before later types that utilized new and more varied means of harnessing energy and putting it to work. The spread of these more advanced forms has pushed the hunting and gathering cultures deeper and deeper into more marginal areas. Today, on the brink of virtual extinction, they are found only in the most harsh and agriculturally unsuitable regions of the world, such as deserts and arctic wastelands. They have, until quite recently, been able to remain viable there because the exploitation of wild food resources yielded a higher energy return per unit of human labor in these environments than any other alternative system available. All of these cultures display a high degree of specialization in the techniques of wresting a livelihood from the limited resources of their hostile environments. For example, the Paiute of Owen's Valley were specialized food collectors to the point where they constructed a network of channels and ditches, some of them being more than a mile long, which served to divert the waters from snow-fed mountain streams and irrigate patches of ground containing wild vegetable resources (Forde 1934: 35–36). Another more dramatic illustration is in the highly specialized, ingenious exploitative techniques of the Eskimo, which have excited the admiration of every investigator who has studied them. In fact, the Eskimo's ecological adaptation is such an effective one that Westerners who have spent any time in the arctic have found it expedient to adopt a good part of the Eskimo's technology.

THE LAW OF CULTURAL DOMINANCE

Our discussion of cultural dominance suggests that a rather broad principle underlies both cases of specific dominance, such as that of recent hunters and gatherers in marginal environments, and the great dominance range of generally advanced cultural forms. We shall call this principle The Law of Cultural Dominance. It may be stated this way: that cultural system which more effectively exploits the energy resources of a given environment will tend to spread in that environment at the expense of less effective systems (cf. Cottrell 1955: 22, 27 for a similar idea). Put another way, the law

75

Evolution and Culture

states that a cultural system will tend to be found precisely in those environments in which it yields a higher energy return per unit of human labor than any alternative system available.

A few brief remarks concerning the law are necessary. First of all, we fully realize that as it stands it offers no measure of a cultural system's thermodynamic effectiveness independently of the fact that it does indeed prevail and tend to spread at the expense of rival systems in a particular environment. This is, of course, a shortcoming, but it could be remedied by developing a usable method of evaluating a cultural system's thermodynamic accomplishment. The fact that few anthropologists have shown any interest in this problem is no indication that such a measure would not be extremely illuminating and valuable in both evolutionary and nonevolutionary studies, or that it cannot be done (see Zimmerman 1951: 61; also Chapter II). In the present state of evolutionary theory we are placed in somewhat the same embarrassing position as the biologists who account for the survival of certain organisms in terms of their better adaptability and then turn about and assert that the reason they know one organism is better adapted to its environment than another is that one survives and the other does not. Despite these logical difficulties, the concept of adaptation has proved to be a very fruitful one and few biologists would be rash enough to maintain that it ought to be discarded. In fact, the fruitfulness of the concept is such—and this is what is really most crucial—that it has led biologists to seek measures of adaptation independent of the rather crude criterion of mere survival. We advance the law of cultural dominance, then, in full awareness of its present drawbacks, with the hope that it will prove to have some utility, and what is more important, with the hope that it will stimulate further thinking and research along these lines.

The second point regarding the law of dominance which should be emphasized is that it refers to dominance in relation to environment. This means that the usual context of its use will be that of specific evolution and that the dominance referred to in such cases is specific dominance. The law also underlies the fact that generally higher cultures have greater dominance range than lower forms, which is to say that it is also relevant to the understanding of general dominance. Higher forms characteristically exploit more different kinds of resources more effectively than lower; hence in most environments they are more effective than lower; thus their greater range. This does not preclude that a particularly well-adapted, highly specialized culture will not be able to maintain specific dominance in its environment, resisting, at least for a time, encroachment of a more advanced and widely dominant culture.

Examples of specific dominance are numerous in the ethnographic literature. Braidwood (1957: 21), for instance, points out that in post-glacial times some of the hunting and gathering societies of western Europe became so specialized and highly adapted in certain ecological zones that they were able to resist for some time incursions by early agricultural systems. A better known illustration of this phenomenon is to be found in aboriginal California. One of the questions which anthropologists have long sought to answer is why there was no agriculture in California in pre-Columbian times. California was adjacent to the agricultural center of the American Southwest so that it is unlikely that isolation or distance could have been a factor preventing the diffusion of agriculture to this area. The topographical features of the state would also seem to be favorable for agricultural production. Our perplexity becomes even greater when we learn that the California Indians were probably not totally ignorant of agricultural techniques since they did raise tobacco. Then how are we to account for the absence of agriculture? Kroeber (1939: 211) has maintained that Native California failed to become agricultural because "of its dry summers, for which, so far as maize was concerned, no amount of winter precipitation could compensate." However, the seasonal distribution of rains does not seem to have prevented the mission Indians during the Spanish occupation of California from producing sizable quantities of maize, in addition to wheat, barley and beans (see Cook 1943: 34–55). Our discussion of cultural dominance suggests another possible explanation which might shed light on the absence of agriculture in aboriginal California.

Kroeber's population figures in his *Cultural and Natural Areas of Native North America* (see Table 18) show that in much of California the density of population was approximately equal to that of the Pueblos: 75 per 100 square kilometers in California and 76 per 100 square kilometers in the Pueblos—which, incidentally, was the highest population density, according to Kroeber, north of the Rio Grande in pre-Columbian times. While the figure of 75 per 100 square kilometers represents the areas of highest population density in California, it is interesting to note that there was no region of California where the density was not appreciably higher than the agricultural area closest to California, the Sonora-Gila-Yuma sphere. The figures are 40 and 39 per 100 square kilometers for the areas marginal to the California climax and 25 and 33 per 100 square kilometers for the entire Sonora-Gila-Yuma area.

78

The Law of Cultural Dominance

Since the regions being discussed are fairly small and since virtually everyone in them was engaged in food-getting activities, the above population density figures may serve as an approximate measure of the relative amounts of energy captured by these cultural systems in their respective environments. It would appear that in the bountiful environment which characterized much of California the energy yield of hunting and gathering activities was truly impressive, and might even have been roughly as high as the energy return of the agricultural systems of the Pueblos. Actually this should not be too astonishing. Both agriculture and wild-food collecting exploit the same energy source, the energy trapped and stored up by plants. The higher thermodynamic potential displayed by agriculture over wild-food collecting in most environments lies not in the fact that it harnesses a new *form* of energy but rather in the greater control it exercises over the same energy source. It is quite conceivable, therefore, that in a particularly generous environment hunting and gathering could yield as much and possibly even more energy than the agricultural systems in other less generous areas. In fact, Kroeber's figures suggest that there was no region of California where hunting and gathering probably did not yield a considerably higher return than did the agriculture of the adjacent Sonora-Gila-Yuma zone.

It is not so difficult, then, to see why hunting and gathering were able to hold their own in California and compete successfully with nearby agricultural systems. The ethnographic evidence indicates that the culture of the California Indians was a well-adapted and highly productive system, specializing in the exploitation of a great variety of abundant wild vegetable and animal resources (Hatt 1953: 161). The fact that agriculture might have yielded an even higher energy return than hunting and gathering in the California environment is beside the point. No society, once it has become well-adapted to its environmental setting, will abandon its way of life and adopt a new one, however more thermodynamically effective the new one may be from some objective standard, unless it is pressured into doing so by outside forces.

The history of the Great Plains of the United States offers an illustration of an environment in which a highly specialized equestrian hunting culture was not only able to hold its own against nearby agricultural systems but actually replace them and spread at their expense. So much of the anthropological interest in the Plains has centered on the colorful horse-riding Indians that the impression is often created that in prehorse days the Plains was just a great cultural vacuum, inhabited only sporadically by a few small groups straying in now and then to do some hunting or perhaps try their hand at a little farming. Archaeological evidence, however, has revealed the important fact that before the introduction of the horse, primitive agriculturalists from the east had pushed far beyond the western borders of the prairies and established themselves in the very heart of the High Plains (Wedel 1941). These agriculturalists can hardly be considered strays since they settled down in permanent villages which were numerous and widespread enough to have left archaeological remains along almost every arable stream valley with a fairly secure water supply as far west as the present state of Colorado.

For our purposes there are a number of facts regarding these prehorse agriculturalists worth noting. First of all, the villages were scattered over much of the choicest bison grounds. Secondly, the agriculture was probably not highly productive since the villages tended to be small and widely dispersed. Wedel (*ibid.*: 15–27) has also commented upon the environmental limitations of agriculture on the Western Plains, although these were not as severe as sometimes has been thought. The diffuse nature of the settlement pattern also suggests that if there were hunting and gathering peoples on the Plains at this time they apparently did not pose much of a military threat to the agriculturalists. This settlement pattern contrasts sharply with that of the agricultural tribes of historic times, such as the Pawnee, who dwelt in a few large, compactly built villages located within a few miles of each other. Naturally these large villages were a great deal more effective for defensive purposes.

By the time the white settlers reached the Plains, the extent of agriculture in the area had been greatly reduced and was found only along its eastern margins. The rest of the Plains was completely dominated by the horse-riding Indians. How then to explain the wholesale abandonment of these numerous farming communities? Wedel (*ibid.*) has suggested that drought conditions might have been a major factor. But why is it necessary to call in the *deus ex machina* of climatic change when we know from historic times that the horse-riding Indians were able to dominate the grasslands and either drive out agriculturalists or transform them into equestrian hunters? It seems more than likely that this is what must have happened to the early agriculturalists on the Western Plains as well. The horse not only provided the equestrian hunters with a tremendous military advantage, but what was probably even more crucial, it supplied them with a more effective means of exploiting the rich biotic resources of the grasslands, yielding a higher energy return than the somewhat precarious agriculture which preceded them. The military superiority of the mounted hunters rested squarely upon a superior material base. This is evidenced by the fact that in those areas where agriculture was more productive, such as along the great river valleys in the eastern margin of the Plains, it was able to hold its own against the rapid spread of the equestrian hunting culture. Even here, however, the rich rewards of the buffalo hunt proved to be an effective lure and the tribes combined agricultural life in settled villages for part of the year with an equestrian hunting life on the surrounding grasslands during the remainder.

Yet the dominance of the equestrian hunters was a short-lived one. Created in large measure by the expansion of European culture across the Atlantic, an offshoot of this same culture shortly thereafter swept them aside, plowed under the buffalo grass, and transformed the Plains into a vast farmland that yielded a much higher energy return than the hunting of the mobile bison herds ever could.

Of course the ultimate historic fate of the aboriginal societies of the Plains was shared to a greater or lesser degree by almost all of the American Indian cultures. From the standpoint of Euroamerican culture, the Indians' exploitation of the continent's rich resources was deemed to be highly inefficient and there was no question but that they had to go. Consequently, the Indian societies were exterminated or driven off and the remainder gathered together and placed on reservations. Tribe after tribe seems to have made a real effort to copy the white ways after being placed on the reservations. Most of them fully realized that the old ways were gone for good and did their best to adapt to the changing currents. But apparently they could not adapt fast enough and so they lost, by one means or another, most of their remaining lands. As one authority on Indian land usage, Walter

Woelke, has written (quoted by Fried 1952: 394): "The Indian lost two-thirds of his reservation lands largely because he could not adapt his culture and economy fast enough to the white methods of exploiting the continental natural resources. Where he made the adaptation, where he proceeded to exploit the natural resources in his possession commercially by and for himself, then he retained possession of his lands."

The only area where the Indian cultures were not completely uprooted and swept aside was the Southwest, a semiarid region which, as Fried (1952: 396) has pointed out, is to such a large extent marginal to the economy of the nation that during World War II it was used by the government for Japanese relocation centers, prisoners-of-war camps, and for a desert training area. In addition it has been the site for a great deal of testing of nuclear weapons. And yet even in the Southwest the material base which made the old ways of life possible has been so greatly undermined by the encroaching dominant culture that it seems but a matter of time before these too go the way of all the other American Indian cultures.

Indian-Euroamerican acculturation in the United States is merely one historic example of the world-wide acculturation process which has been set in motion by the rise and spread of a new dominant culture type, this time a culture type whose range of general dominance is so great that it is spreading to just about every ecological nook and cranny of the planet.

Advanced cultural systems are no less bound by the imperatives of adapting to their environment than less advanced cultural systems, although the fact that they can adapt to a much wider variety of environments has often created the impression that they are somehow freer in this respect. The law of cultural dominance, therefore, underlies with equal rigor the historic movements of more complex cultures as it does those of simpler cultures. Probably one of its clearest illustrations is the rise and spread of Chinese culture.

China was a complex civilization based upon an intensive agricultural economy made even more intensive by the construction of large-scale public works in irrigation, drainage, and transport by a widespread network of canals. All this made possible the production of a grain surplus, the concentration and redistribution of which determined the concentration of political power (Chi 1934).

The major direction of the expansion of Chinese culture was always toward the south rather than the north. Fanning out from the Yellow River Valley, Chinese culture moved relentlessly southward—in times of dynastic disintegration as well as imperial unification—engulfing lands, peoples, and cultures and putting the permanent and unmistakable stamp of "Chinese" on them. Those people that could not be assimilated were either driven off into less desirable areas of exploitation or exterminated. To the south lay the richly fertile Yangtze River Valley permitting the highly intensive system of agriculture upon which Chinese culture rested, so that there were few barriers to expansion in this direction. But to the north lay the great ecological cleavage separating the river basins of China with its intensive agriculture and the poorly watered steppe region with its extensive pastoral economy. In this direction the expansion of Chinese culture was consistently frustrated.

Throughout Chinese history, the northern frontier separating Chinese from barbarian continued to be a factor of great significance. World history is replete with instances of barbarians from beyond the pale who come down on a nearby civilization like "the wolf on the fold," only to be transformed in the process toward the cultural image of those they had defeated. China is perhaps the classic example of this phenomenon since it occurred there so repeatedly. Time and again China was conquered from across the northern frontier by the mounted nomads of the steppes. But tribal penetration too far south of the frontier, no matter how great the initial military strength, always resulted in the eventual Sinicization of the invaders. To conquer China militarily was one thing, but once it had been vanquished many nomad chieftains learned, as one of the Chinese statesmen put it, that "China cannot be ruled on horseback." The nomads fully recognized and appreciated the material superiority of Chinese culture and were only too eager to exploit it. To do this, however, they had to abandon the very organization which had made the conquest possible in the first place and were forced to perpetuate almost the whole of Chinese culture—all of which bears out Lattimore's remark (1938: 15): "It is the poor nomad who is the pure nomad."

The ability of Chinese culture to absorb and Sinicize all barbarian invaders that came within its environmental borders is well-known. The converse, however, was equally true. Outside of these environmental borders the thermodynamic superiority of Chinese culture was lost and other systems of exploitation proved to be more effective. Therefore, every attempt made by Chinese culture, no matter how strong the ruling dynasty at the time, to extend its range of dominance too far beyond the northern frontier resulted in the outlying Chinese taking to pastoral nomadism, becoming tribalized and eventually turning inward on China as so-called barbarians. The crucial factor in the development of steppe nomads

85

on the fringe of North China was, as Lattimore has pointed out (1947: 36): ". . . not the development of the technique of domestication, but the point of economic pressure on the marginal land at the edge of the steppe at which the use of a few square miles of steppe for grazing became convincingly more profitable than the use of a few drought-harried acres for agriculture. Once this point was reached, people began to abandon their farms in significantly large numbers, and take off into the steppe as full nomads."

Both the written and archaeological evidence available indicates that pastoral nomadism did not originate in the heart of the steppe lands but along its outer margins (*ibid.*: 33). Beardsley (1953) has pointed up the critical role that the invention of horse riding played in the development of the pastoral economy. In its spread across the steppes pastoralism was able to draw into its orbit and transform into typical nomads not only marginal farmers from China's northern frontier, but also marginal farmers from the oases and uncertain watercourses of Inner Asia, forest hunters from the northern fringes of the steppes, as well as people from other surrounding areas. Like the culture of the Plains Indians, pastoral nomadism was a highly adapted cultural system which specialized in exploiting the resources of the steppes. It is true that in certain sectors of the steppelands there were ecological niches which did favor the formation of other kinds of cultural systems. These included varying combinations of pastoral nomadism, hunting, agriculture and town life. However, the extent of the area which favored the life of the steppe herdsman was so much greater than that of the areas favoring other systems of exploitation that pastoral nomadism never lost its ascendancy over these other cultural forms. Within its environmental domain pastoral nomadism was able to maintain a specific dominance for numerous centuries and effectively resist all attempts at encroachment by nearby and more advanced agricultural systems. It is only in recent years, with the spread of a new dominant culture type, industrialism, to Asia that the ancient ecological and cultural cleavage between steppe and sown is finally being obliterated.

MECHANISMS OF DOMINANCE

How does a more effective culture type actually dominate and transform less effective types?

Every cultural system, once all the potentialities inherent in its level of organization have reached a limit and it has achieved a satisfactory adaptation to its environment, will tend to become stabilized. It then becomes difficult for it to totally readapt. Of course the system will be able to accommodate certain changes from the outside but only so long as its basic adaptation is not thereby jeopardized. This would appear to be the underlying basis of what anthropologists have often called the natural "conservatism of culture." To illustrate what we mean: as noted earlier in connection with the California Indians, a hunting and gathering people whose culture is well-adapted to exploiting the wild food resources of a particular area is not likely to voluntarily abandon food collecting and adopt agriculture, even though from some objective standard the cultivation of plants might yield a higher energy return in that environment.

It would seem, then, that the spread of a dominant culture type almost invariably involves some sort of pressure being brought to bear on less advanced types. Often this pressure takes the extreme form of outright military conquest with the conquered society being exterminated, driven off, or colonized and transformed. The mechanics of this process are easily understood. In most cases, an advanced cultural system can marshal a greater and more powerfully equipped military force, enabling it to take, and hold against encroachment or revolt, areas where its exploitative techniques are more effective than rival systems.

Sometimes it is the pressure created by the threat of possible conquest or extermination which is enough to bring about the spread of a dominant type. For example, after the mounted hunting of the bison herds became the dominant culture type on the Great Plains of the United States, many of the agricultural village tribes on the eastern fringe of the Plains, in order to avoid being wiped out entirely, took wholly or partially to equestrian hunting. Thus they came to approach, more or less, the typical Plains culture type.

A dominant type may sometimes be spread by a less advanced form which is actively resisting the political and economic domination of a more advanced form. This is certainly a common enough occurrence in our own day; we read almost daily of nationalistic movements sweeping across the so-called underdeveloped countries of the world. Many of these nationalistic movements have indeed been successful, but their success has to a very great extent been dependent upon their using the ideology, political forms and even some of the industrial techniques of the same societies they are trying to resist. In the very process of defending the integrity of their political boundaries against the domination of advanced powers their culture is transformed, more closely approaching that of the dominant type.

The appearance of nationalistic movements and other political forms in areas where the technological concomitants of these forms are absent illustrates a cultural phenomenon which has been noted by many social scientists, but about which there seems to be a great deal of confusion. We refer to the fact that in the spread of more advanced culture types very often the ideological component will tend to spread farther and faster than its technological component. It is not difficult to see why this occurs. The more advanced the culture type the more complex is the technology. In the most advanced cultures of the present day the technological base has become an enormously complex affair, requiring sizable amounts of capital, specialized skills, organization, and great quantities of raw materials to develop it and keep it going—all of which means that it can be transmitted across cultural boundaries only with the greatest difficulty. Ideological elements, on the other hand, even those of the most advanced cultures, can be carried across cultural boundaries with relative ease.

But there is a further reason why the ideological component of advanced cultural systems has tended to spread more rapidly than its technological component. The great complexity of highly evolved technological systems has made it possible for advanced societies to discourage and hinder its spread. They have, on the other hand, not only been unable to prevent the spread of its ideological concomitant but in many cases they have actually fostered it. All of the European colonial powers, for instance, used their political, financial and economic power to prevent, or at least slow down as far as possible, the spread of industrialism to the less advanced countries under their political control because they were primarily interested in markets and sources of raw materials and not in creating manufacturing competitors. The French were characteristically quite frank about this: as Charles Robequain observed (quoted by Sternberg 1950: 41), "The free development of industry has never been allowed in any colony; even the possibility of such development was long considered paradoxical, almost inconceivable, by the mother country." Although written explicitly about the French colonies, this statement would accurately describe the policy of all the European colonial powers.

The attempts made by the European powers to insulate their colonies from other aspects of Western Culture besides the technological proved to be less successful. The colonial areas had to be politically administered and economically exploited. This meant transplanting many of the political and ideological concomitants of an industrial technology to these societies at the very same time that they were preventing, or retarding, the spread of the technology itself. It is for this reason that the colonial areas of the world exhibit what might be called a partial cultural dominance. Japan is an instructive case because she is the exception that proves the rule, so to speak. The Japanese learned their lesson quickly and they learned it well. They had stood to one side and carefully observed the rest of Asia being carved up and apportioned by the various European powers. Japan really had very little choice in the matter; it was industrialize or be gobbled up like the rest. She therefore industrialized. The fact that Japan was never colonized by any of the European powers was of crucial importance in her industrial development, since it permitted industrialism to spread to Japan without running head on into the sort of barriers erected by the European powers in colonized portions of Asia.

It is understandable, then, why social scientists investigating particular societies in various areas of the world, especially those in colonial areas, have often discovered that the ideological components of industrial cultures have preceded the technological. Such seeming developmental anomalies are encountered as the "Protestant Ethic" turning up among the natives of Melanesia, or communities in the less advanced areas of the world "choosing progress," or newly created nations such as Ghana exhibiting many of the political forms of a nation state and yet lacking the underpinning of a national economy. These societies give the impression of being built like the famous houses in *Gulliver's Travels*, from the roof down. They have frequently been cited as evidence in support of the thesis that ideology is often the prime mover in the evolution of culture. The confusion here lies in the failure to distinguish between the origin of a cultural phenomenon and its spread to some particular society. From a general evolutionary perspective, an industrial technology gives rise to an appropriate social system and ideology. It does not follow, however, that in the spread of these various components they will necessarily reach less advanced societies in that respective order. The actual sequence in which they do reach less advanced societies will depend on a variety of selective factors, some of which we have mentioned in the previous pages.

To summarize: general evolutionary advance in both the organic and cultural realms has been achieved by a succession of dominant types each of which has embodied more varied and effective means of exploiting the energy resources of a greater variety of environments, and as a result has tended to spread at the expense of previous types. Although the more advanced types display a greater range of dominance it does not mean that they will be able to dominate in all specific environments. It sometimes happens that some forms at the lower levels become so highly adapted and specialized in exploiting the resources of some particular habitat that they are able to maintain a specific dominance in that environment and resist incursions by more widely dominant types. Thus higher and lower types may continue to exist side by side. In the organic world, because of the enormous variety of ecological niches, this situation may persist indefinitely. But the varieties of ecological niches that can be filled by cultural systems are so few by comparison, and the range of dominance of the most recent and advanced type has become so great, that the diversity of cultural types has been steadily reduced. It seems merely a matter of time before all of the cultural systems of the world will be different variations, depending upon divergent historical experiences, of a single culture type.

The law of cultural dominance, which is derived from examination of the process of the rise and spread of dominant culture types, not only underlies the distribution of cultures and the historic movements of peoples and societies, but also explains why some cultural systems have been able to spread at the expense of others and why some have not. Actually, the significance of the factor of cultural dominance has been noted and emphasized by a number of scholars in a variety of historical contexts. Fried's essay (1952) comparing culture contact in the United States and China, Barth's recent discussion of ecological relationships of ethnic groups in North Pakistan (1956), and Lattimore's work on the cultures of Inner Asia (1940), are all studies in which cultural dominance, although not always called this, figures prominently. What we have attempted to do in this essay, however, is to give a name to this phenomenon and to formulate a general proposition, related to the evolutionary process as a whole, which would embrace all the historical examples.

The Law of Evolutionary Potential

The mid-century revival of interest in cultural evolutionism in anthropology seems to be a limited and one-sided
one so far, concerned almost exclusively with problems of
specific adaptation. Presumably, too, a large number of
anthropologists remain uncommitted even to this. At any
rate, evolutionism in its general as well as specific aspects
needs further explication, especially in the context of its
applications. A remark frequently made by anthropologists is that they want to be shown how evolutionary
theory can be *used* before they pass judgment on it. This,
we think, is a perfectly fair requirement.

In previous chapters the characteristics of evolution
have been treated separately, in the context of "other
things being equal." Each factor by itself has been shown
to have some uses in the explanation of certain kinds of
cultural events, but it must be recognized that a consideration of only one factor at a time imposes limitations
on explanation, for the "other things" are not often constant in nature. All are actually in complex interplay and
therefore variable in their effects in particular times,
places, or circumstances.

In order to test our ability to explain and predict the
evolutionary progress of specific populations and cultures, we must first define the expectable results of the

various evolutionary processes in their interaction. Once these relationships have been discussed generally we shall attempt various interpretations with them. The illustrations will range diversely from some simple anthropological problems of the primitive world to the complex question of the modern and future world and America's place in it.

One of the virtues of the evolutionary view is that, more than any other perspective, it makes the concerns of cultural anthropology directly relevant to modern life and to the future. As Tylor once put it, it is the "knowledge of man's course of life, from the remote past to the present," the study of the *evolution* of culture, that will enable us to forecast the future. The modern social sciences, now that they are almost exclusively nontemporal, or functional, have not been able to help us to judge the future and thus guide our actions and deliberations in relation to modern political problems. The past-as-related-to-the-future has long since been left to dogmatic Marxists or to the more respectable but nevertheless equally nonscientific "universal" historians such as Brooks Adams, Spengler, Huntington, and Toynbee.

Let us briefly review those characteristics of evolution that we now want to consider as interrelated phenomena. First, it has been noted that evolution can be regarded as a double-faceted phenomenon. On the one hand any given system—a species, a culture, or an individual—improves its chances for survival, progresses in the efficiency of energy capture, by increasing its adaptive specialization. This is specific evolution. The obverse is directional advance or progress stage by stage, measured in absolute terms rather than by criteria relative to the degree of adaptation to particular environments. The systems also are assigned to stages irrespective of their phylogenetic relationship. A man is higher than an armadillo; yet they are each adapted differently and are contemporary species and members of different lines of descent. This is general evolution.

We have also seen that there is a limiting factor inherent in specific evolution. This has been called the Principle of Stabilization, and it occurs as an end product of adaptation. Specific evolution means increasing adaptation to an environment, which is to say that it ultimately becomes nonprogressive. Because adaptation is self-limiting at some point, if all of the forms of life and culture were to become fully adapted, evolution, whether viewed specifically or generally, would halt.

The fact of the matter is, of course, that evolution continues precisely because new forms come into being which are *not* highly specialized. Some of these more generalized mutants have a potential for new kinds of adaptation or adaptation to new kinds of environments. Thus we have the contradictory-sounding propositions: the evolution of species takes place *because of* adaptation; the evolution of the total system of life takes place *in spite of* adaptation.

Another factor, the dominance which a higher species may exert over lower species, tends to be the most effective inhibitor of any potential that may reside in an unspecialized species. Much of the struggle and warfare that is endemic in both the world of biology and of culture can be interpreted as the contest between the dominance factor and the potentiality factor. This also may be phrased in contradictory-sounding statements: specific evolution is a movement from homogeneity to heterogeneity, from few to more species; yet one of the frequent consequences of evolution is the movement from heterogeneity toward homogeneity, as a higher dominant form such as man spreads at the expense of lower forms.

These ideas should not be unfamiliar to anyone conversant with recent literature on biological evolution. Julian Huxley, in particular, has pointed out that evolution is not a straight line of progress from one highly developed species to the next highest but that it proceeds in zigzag fashion as advances are countered by stabilization or dominance, that limitation is as likely as improvement. Most relevant to the present discussion is the recognition that what Simpson has called "opportunism" for evolutionary advance exists as a better possibility for a more generalized form than for the specialized, well-adapted and therefore stabilized one. As Huxley put it (1943: 500): ". . . the further a trend toward specialization has proceeded, the deeper will be the biological groove in which [the species] has thus entrenched itself." Or again (*ibid.*: 562): ". . . there is no certain case on record of a line showing a high degree of specialization giving rise to a new type. All new types which themselves are capable of adaptive radiation seem to have been produced by relatively unspecialized ancestral lines."

One of the main purposes of this chapter is to show that this characteristic of biological evolution is expectable in the evolution of culture as well. Further, we wish to state the proposition in the form of a law—that is, to affirm its generality as explicitly as possible. It has been introduced in the context of biological evolution in order to argue for its acceptability as an idea; evolutionary ideas expressed in biological terms seem to find readier acceptance than they do in cultural terms. But this should not be taken to mean that the idea began in biology and that now it is simply being carried over into the cultural context. As we shall see, there are evidences of its prior realization, incipiently at least, by students of cultural phenomena.

The law, which may be called The Law of Evolutionary Potential, is a simple one: The more specialized and adapted a form in a given evolutionary stage, the smaller is its potential for passing to the next stage. Another way of putting it which is more succinct and more in conformity with preceding chapters is: Specific evolutionary progress is inversely related to general evolutionary potential.

It is important to remember that because of the stabilization of specialized species and because new advances occur in less specialized species, over-all progress is characteristically irregular and discontinuous rather than a direct line from one advanced species to its next descendant. Instead of continuing the advance related species diverge as they specialize and adapt. This discontinuity, which now seems obvious, has been usually overlooked as a significant feature of the evolutionary process. Evolution is usually diagrammed as a tree with the trunk representing the "main line" of progress, as though the advance from the highest form at one stage to the new form at the next were phylogenetically continuous. It is an inappropriate and misleading picture, however, and the recognition of the discontinuity of advance is an important element in the understanding of some major problems. (See p. 17 for a better diagram.)

We are not sure where the lineal view of evolution came from, but it has been a mischievous one. The difficulty it has caused in anthropology has been discussed in Chapter II, but here it may be well to remark that there has been a much more pervasive confusion than that. Hegel's "dialectical" conception of evolution is a special version of the lineal view and when it was adopted by Marx and Engels and ultimately became part of a political dogma, the error was widespread as well as resistant to any arguments against it. According to Hegel, *everything*, including society and even human nature, is in a state of evolution; everything carries within itself the forces which change it. Never mind the famous "negations" that cause the revolutionary leaps; what is at issue now is Hegel's "flux," the idea that each and every system of things evolves as a self-contained unit. There is no phylogenetic discontinuity and no sound idea of variable potentiality in the Hegelian view. This fault is what led Marx, Engels, and others to presume that the revolution which would usher in the new stage of industrial socialism would occur in the most *advanced* industrial countries—that evolution proceeds from the most advanced form on to the next level. But when the Bolsheviks won in Russia, a most unlikely place from the Hegel-Marx point of view, the Marxists became confused. When expediency led Lenin and then Stalin to retain power in Russia no matter what the theory said, many others, "pure Marxists," rejected the Bolsheviks and formed the numerous splinter parties that exist to this day as opponents of Stalinism. What a lot of assassinations a mere theory can cause! Perhaps this is a sufficient answer to those who say that evolutionary laws are so general that they are meaningless.

In order to emphasize the nonlineal nature of progress, we shall state two new principles, obvious aspects of the law of potential. One could be called the Phylogenetic Discontinuity of Progress. It would mean only what was stated above, that an advanced form does not normally beget the next stage of advance; that the next stage begins in a different line.

Because species tend to occupy a given territory continuously, another obvious derivative principle suggests itself. This may be called the Local Discontinuity of Progress. It means merely that if successive stages of progress are not likely to go from one species to its next descendant, then they are not likely to occur in the same locality. As we shall see, this principle is especially appropriate for studies of cultural evolution because we so frequently name a culture after the territory in which it is found.

No one has completely or succinctly formulated any of these laws but several writers have come close. Two in particular have discussed and used rather similar ideas in specific interpretations. They are Thorstein Veblen and Leon Trotsky.

Veblen's analysis of Imperial Germany makes considerable use of two ideas reminiscent of the above discussion. One is that Germany became more efficient industrially than her predecessor, England, because of "the merits of borrowing"; the other is that England, conversely, was finally less efficient than Germany because of "the penalty of taking the lead" (1915: esp. Chapters II–IV). Later, Trotsky, in his *History of the Russian Revolution* formulated the idea somewhat more aptly. He used one particularly luminous phrase: "the privilege of historic backwardness." In the context of his discussion this means that an "underdeveloped" civilization has certain evolutionary potentials that an advanced one lacks. He put it this way (nd: 4–5):

Although compelled to follow after the advanced countries, a backward country does not take things in the same order. The privilege of historic backwardness—and such a privilege exists—permits, or rather compels, the adoption of whatever is ready in advance of any specified date, skipping a whole series of intermediate stages.

Trotsky went on to develop his idea and to formulate it as The Law of Combined Development (*ibid.:* 9):

The law of combined development reveals itself most indubitably . . . in the history and character of Russian industry. Arising late, Russian industry did not repeat the development of the advanced countries, but inserted itself into this development, adapting their latest achievements to its own backwardness. Just as the economic evolution of Russia as a whole skipped over the epoch of craft-guilds and manufacture, so also the separate branches of industry made a series of special leaps over technical productive stages that had been measured in the West by decades. Thanks to this, Russian industry developed at certain periods with extraordinary speed.

Several writers prior to Veblen and Trotsky, including Lewis H. Morgan, had remarked on the tendency of backward societies to skip over whole stages of development by borrowing from the culture of advanced societies, but no one has been so explicit as Trotsky about the *potentiality* of backwardness, nor so daring as to propose it as a scientific law. The emphasis on diffusion in Trotsky's argument (as suggested in the phrase "combined development") and in Veblen's idea of the "merits of borrowing" calls attention to an important feature of the evolutionary process in culture which does not have its analogue in biological evolution. The lack of any possible connection between species except the genetic makes convergence in biological evolution a rarer phenomenon, and also makes specific evolution a slower, more gradual, and more connected series of changes than in the diffusional continuum of culture. This difference, nevertheless, does not alter the applicability of the law of evolutionary potential to both biology and culture.

Other writers have commented on the converse of the notion of the privilege of backwardness, that there is a stagnation and lack of potentiality inherent in highly developed cultures.

That very wise Frenchman, Alexis de Tocqueville, over 100 years ago made an interesting statement concerning the potentiality of the U.S.A. and Russia as compared with the stabilization of the more developed nations (1954: 2, 452). He wrote:

> There are at the present time two great nations in the world which seem to tend toward the same end, although they started from different points; I allude to the Russians and the Americans. Both of them have grown up unnoticed; and while the attention of mankind was directed elsewhere, they have suddenly assumed a prominent place among the nations; and the world learned their existence and their greatness at almost the same time. All other nations seem to have nearly reached their natural limits . . . but these are still in the act of growth; all others are stopped, or continue to advance with extreme difficulty . . .

Arnold Toynbee is also concerned with this historical stop-and-go, leapfrogging character of progress and addresses it as a central problem, but his anthropocentric, psychologistic perspective prevents him from seeing any nonmental process at work. All of the historians concerned with the phenomenon usually called "the rise and fall of civilizations" could have made good use of the law of evolutionary potential. It could have, for example, made Spengler's and Brooks Adams' conceptions of "decline" and "decay" more comprehensible.

Another historian, H. Stuart Hughes, has written a provocative essay called "The Twentieth Century Byzantium" (1949), expanding the subject of cultural stabilization and conservatism. Hughes says (as others have) that the U.S.A. is to Western Europe as Rome was to Greece; that as a later but more primitive offshoot of an older civilization, the U.S.A., like Rome, raised certain aspects of that civilization to new levels of efficiency and specialization. He then goes on to stress that the U.S.A. is now stabilized and coming to occupy a conservative position in the world, more like the later Byzantium than Rome itself. One wishes that Professor Hughes had formulated his idea in more general evolutionary terms. As it is, the law of evolutionary potential is practically at the point of his pen.

The failure of so many historians, including such anthropological culture-historians as A. L. Kroeber, to formulate such a law even when they seem to be purposely seeking a general statement is probably because they *are* historians, by profession and commitment nonevolutionists, whereas the explanation for the variable potentiality for civilizational advance among different kinds of cultures stems logically only from evolutionary theory. Happily for this argument, both Veblen and Trotsky can be considered evolutionists.

One feels a little foolish in proclaiming a scientific law inasmuch as it is done so frequently as a form of humor. There are certain advantages to this procedure, however, which are greater than the risks. But first it must be admitted that all of the illustrations to follow, and a thousand more, would not prove that the law of evolutionary potential is "true." A law states a relationship between two (or more) classes of phenomena, as this one has done with respect to general evolution and specific adaptation, but always it must be understood that other factors are regarded as constant. In nature, however, there are no constants. A law can be proved true only with laboratory apparatus which can keep all factors controlled, and of course many scientific laws cannot be submitted to laboratory tests. The criterion in these cases becomes not truth in the absolute sense, but their explanatory value. A law is a law if it is useful, if it renders particular events more understandable by showing them to be instances of an already comprehended general phenomenon. As Morris Cohen put it, "the repeatable escapes us if it is not identified."

THE LAW ILLUSTRATED

The foregoing discussion of history shows that there has been for some time a nearly recognized utility for the law of evolutionary potential in the realm of civilizational phenomena, in these cases European history specifically. But if it is a *general* law of evolution it should be useful in any and all kinds of situations that involve the evolutionary process. It requires but a little reflection to accumulate numerous examples of the operation of the law and its corollaries.

The evolution of writing in the ancient Mediterranean provides one of the more simple and obvious instances. The Egyptian system of combined hieroglyphic and rebus writing was the most advanced and specialized example of that stage. Imbedded in it were a few suggestions of a new phase, certain symbols that stood for syllables and some even for a few single phonetic sounds. But so fixed were they in the cumbersome Egyptian system, and so adjusted was the total system to the rest of Egyptian culture, that the potentiality of the phonetic elements could not be realized there. Instead, the much more effective and economical alphabetic system emerged elsewhere, among East Mediterranean peoples (some say the Phoenicians) who had *no writing at all* and who could, therefore, make a fresh start with only the most appropriate and efficient elements from the old composite system.

Science itself, because it is such a clear case of evolutionary progress, is full of examples of the law of evolutionary potential. We see not only local (or national) discontinuity in the development of science, but also a sort of phylogenetic discontinuity—which may be more precisely described in this case as generational discontinuity. Young scientists tend to surpass their elders, when other things such as brains, of course, are equal. The well-established individuals ordinarily do not go on making successive important contributions because they become so committed, adapted, to a particular line of thought. The young are generalized and unstable, in a sense, and have the "privilege of backwardness" which enables them to appropriate only the more fruitful and progressive of the older generation's accomplishments, disregarding or discarding as useless debris much of the work that went on before them.

If the law of evolutionary potential is a good law, if it corresponds closely enough to what actually happens in nature so that predictions can be made from it, then we should find that the *faster* a science or civilization or whatever kind of system is evolving the *more* discontinuous will be the character of the advance. Thus we see that physics, which has been progressing of late more rapidly than most other sciences, is also characterized by greater discontinuity. The generational discontinuity is particularly striking; very young people, however heavily bearded, seem to win most of the prizes. (In this connection, by the way, some practical advice may be adduced: when medical science is advancing rapidly, as it seems to be right now, go to a *young* doctor.)

The leapfrogging of age by youth can even characterize whole societies if the total culture is evolving fast enough. In the older stabilized cultures, youth is subordinated to age; the older the person, the wiser and more respected he becomes. But in rapid change, youth is served, and the experienced elders, adapted to the outmoded cultural forms, become merely old fogeys. In the past, our disrespect for age has been a most noticeable characteristic of the U.S.A. to European visitors. Lately we hear of the "cult of youth" in Russia and China, as might be expected.

The next illustrations are chosen in order to describe the possible predictive and explanatory value of the law in specific kinds of researches. At this point, it is argued that it may be fruitfully employed by archaeologists.

It has been regarded as anomalous that in Mesoamerica ancestral stages to the High Culture have not been found in the same regions as the High Culture, that there are no nearby underlying stages more primitive than the so-called Middle Culture. But if the law of evolutionary potential is applicable to the Mesoamerican situation then we should not expect to find preceding *stages* necessarily linked to the latest in the same area. The succession from the Middle to the High Culture is expectable as an instance of specific evolution, gradual progress in adaptive specialization within the stage. The great leap in progress from a hunting-gathering stage to the fully agricultural stage of the Middle Culture would presumably follow the principle of local discontinuity; the early periods of the advance probably occurred in a different place from the later phases. The principle of local discontinuity, of course, does not spell out the location, but does help dispel the puzzlement felt because the transitional period seems to be absent from the areas of the later development.

As a general rule, we may say that within any particular culture, or with respect to a particular people or locality, any evidences of a *continuum* of progressive changes are likely to represent development within a single historic line. But a sudden leap forward is apt to be accomplished by a different, relatively unspecialized culture; rapid advance would appear as a historical or phylogenetic discontinuity.

The more-or-less legendary history of the arrival of successive invasions of "barbarians" in Central Mexico is a good illustration of this latter point. The Toltecs, Chichimecs, and Aztecs were each a primitive, helpless group of newcomers at first, compared to the established occupants of the region. But this was an evolutionary privilege, and they in turn rapidly rose to dominate their locality and beyond by combining in their own development the most effective aspects of the culture around them. And the last shall be first.

Here is another example relevant to archaeology. Botanists have argued that the origin of agriculture in the Americas was probably in the tropical forests. What has the law of evolutionary potential to say to this? First, we note that the fertile grasslands and savannahs were probably the areas of the most productive hunting and gathering and the virgin tropical forests probably very poor because the light-denying canopy of high vegetation prevents the growth of forage at ground level. The likely result would be that the most highly developed and dominant bands would live in the grasslands, the most backward and helpless would be pushed into the tropical forests. Because the most successfully adapted have the least potential for advancing into a new stage, we have here a suggestion from evolutionary theory, then, that the botanical argument for the forest origin of agriculture may be correct. The words "suggestion" and "may" are used above in order to avoid the implication that a question of particular historical fact is decided by citing the law. It merely suggests a likelihood, in effect like that of the botanical conjectures themselves; a theory may be helpful in the absence of full factual knowledge but it is not a substitute for that knowledge.

Something like the above situation has been described by V. Gordon Childe in his discussion of the beginnings of the Neolithic in the Old World. As he put it (1946: 41): "The [Neolithic] revolutionaries were not the most advanced savages of the Old Stone Age—the Magdalenians were all too successfully specialized for exploiting the pleistocene environment—but humbler groups who had created less specialized and less brilliant cultures farther south."

The relevance of the law to the so-called "rise and fall of civilization" has already been mentioned, but this phenomenon is such a good example of a grand-scaled problem that its classical manifestation in the Mediterranean region might well be considered a little further. Here was rise and fall beautifully illustrated. A sudden and unprecedented precipitation of culture into the level of true civilization occurred somewhere in Mesopotamia and this civilization then diffused widely in the Fertile Crescent. But then it differentiated, adapted, and became stabilized, with local peculiarities and at higher levels in some places like Babylon and Egypt, and lower in others. Yet even these high levels finally fell behind the advance of newly civilized Greece. Then upstart Rome, which began in tribal organization and *was* built in a day, figuratively speaking, advanced over Greece only to be surpassed later by the Arabs and finally Northern Europe.

There is much to be said—and much has been said— about all this history, but "rise and fall" has remained unexplained. It appears that what should be considered merely a set of instances of the law of evolutionary potential, or more precisely of the corollary principle of local discontinuity, and thus a wholly expectable phenomenon, has been mystifying historians for a long time. Despite the great ingenuity put into the studies and the great piling up of fact, the explanations offered are mere verbal devices like "challenge and response," "withdrawal and return," "concentration and dispersion," "youth and senescence," "growth and fatigue," "the failure of nerve," "decadence," "overeating," and so on. A famous economic historian varies from these only slightly when he cites "economic growth and economic decline" (Clough 1951).

All this is not to say that there are no more problems in the study of the rise and fall of the classical civilizations, but if the fact that evolutionary advance is locally discontinuous is regarded as abnormal and therefore requiring special explanation, then great labors lead to no results. If, on the other hand, we consider the discontinuity of advance and the relatively greater potential for advance of the backward areas over the more developed as normal and expectable in evolution, then that aspect of the rise-and-fall problem is not a problem. That which is to be explained is the exception to the law, not the more numerous instances that conform to the law.

Now that the examples being used here have moved to the level of civilization, we may appropriately continue on to modern times. This is at some risk, it must be admitted, because we all tend to lose perspective and to become influenced by political dogmas when we deal with contemporary problems. But let us first discuss China, a prime example of a huge and complex civilization which, although contemporary, is nevertheless an "old" one, quite backward from the standpoint of modern industrial civilization.

Japan, once a poor cultural relative of China, moved into the modern industrial stage of coal and oil energy and became dominant in the Far East. Partly, this could occur because of the potentiality of its backwardness and "newness" as opposed to the great inertia of the ancient, highly adapted and specialized agricultural civilization of China. Partly, too, Japan was free to advance because she was relatively independent of the dominance that Western civilization exerted over China. But now, perhaps paradoxically from the point of view of Japan, China has greater potential for moving into the new and radically different industrial stage to be based on the electronic storage and transmission of such new sources of power as atomic and direct solar energy. China is not nearly so adapted as Japan to the present and soon-to-be-outmoded industrial complex of coal and oil energy.

Mao Tse-tung has commented on this outlook in picturesque language:

Apart from other characteristics, our people of over 600 million souls is characterized by poverty and by a vacuity which is like that of a sheet of blank paper. This may seem to be a bad thing, whereas in reality it is a good one. . . . Nothing is written on a sheet of paper which is still blank, but it lends itself admirably to receive the latest and most beautiful words and the latest and most beautiful pictures. (Quoted by Bettelheim 1959: 458.)

The potentiality of large nonindustrialized areas like China is great even in relatively small matters. As China borrows the alphabet she could make it a phonemic one. She could have simplified rules of spelling. She could institute a metric system of weights and measures. As she begins the manufacture of typewriters they could be built with a keyboard scientifically arranged for the spelling of the language rather than following our own illogical one, and so on. Improvements in all of these matters and many others are already known to us, but our civilization seems unable to use them because of the prior commitment to earlier forms, whereas China should have less difficulty.

THE PRESENT AND FUTURE OF AMERICA

Now we have arrived at a point where it is inescapable logic that if the law of evolutionary potential can be used to interpret the past or to discuss a non-Western civilization, then it must be relevant to an interpretation of the present and to predictions of future trends, not only of non-Western civilizations but of our own as well.

Some social scientists might reject this use of scientific theory on the grounds that it becomes "political," while in the meantime they occupy themselves with such contemporary problems as those of personnel management, vocational guidance, buyers' preferences, or how to facilitate the washing of our own brains by improved communications theory and motivation research. We feel, however, that while scientific findings, facts or theories, may be politically *relevant* it does not follow that they are "political," if this means that they somehow become nonscientific. For modern science to contribute something, however little, to a comprehension of the major problems of the world is certainly for the good of civilization. This presumes that the findings derive from truly detached scientific interests, as the present argument has, rather than from ideological commitments to a political platform, or from a desire to be of immediate practical service, or from some other personal motivations.

Frequently the major problem of Western civilization is phrased in terms of fear for the future of this speck in the cosmos, a fear that we all may be consumed in an atomic holocaust. As William Faulkner put it, "Our tragedy today is a general and universal physical fear so long sustained by now that we can even bear it." Certainly such a fear is justified, particularly now that some drunken or suicidal master sergeant could precipitate the launching of the horror weapons, and it is small comfort to believe that some portion of mankind could still survive: ". . . that when the last ding-dong of doom has clanged and faded from the last worthless rock hanging tideless in the last red and dying evening, that even then there will still be one more sound: that of his puny inexhaustible voice, still talking."

About an accidental war there is nothing to predict or vouchsafe from the evolutionary perspective. There we can only hope, or with other citizens cry to the military to please be careful, or write postcards to a congressman asking for the outlawing of nuclear weapons. But about a war of calculation, a war resulting from aims and policy and knowledge, there is something to say. The terms of peace treaties show clearly that wars are fought not out of anger, from a desire to exterminate the enemy—however much the battle cries may sound like it—but for certain specific objectives. If nobody is likely to win *anything*, however, and if generals, presidents, and dictators and their families are exposed to death along with lesser citizens, then we may not reasonably expect a purposely incited thermonuclear war. But there is a terrible danger that small, local skirmishes and revolutions in other areas might eventually involve the major powers, and here we come to the point where we may speak relevantly of the nature of the rest of the world, of the position of Western civilization with respect to it, and of what we may logically expect of the future so that we might argue for a realistic policy.

Other sciences have taught us that there are now several new ways to harness energy, powers ultimately of enormous magnitude and very cheap. This power future is to encompass not only the well-known energy from atom-splitting and fusion, but from direct sunlight, from the sea, from new kinds of agriculture, and so on. But as common sense as well as the only slightly more recondite law of evolutionary potential could tell us, those nations that are now the most advanced in the present coal and oil complex have less potential for the full and efficient use of the industry of the future than certain hitherto "underdeveloped" regions which could build a new civilization well adapted to such a base. It is Marxian justice, perhaps even poetic justice, that because of her "premature revolution" Russia is already so committed to the present form of industry that she might be eclipsed by a still newer industrial region.

The future of the U.S.A. may be analogous to the "decline and fall" of others earlier, in the classic period of the Mediterranean world. But the word "fall" has unfortunate connotations. We need not be exterminated, or even overrun as was Rome. Perhaps we might hope to comport ourselves like the Greeks after Rome became dominant: to become an aristocratic people, austere and unimpressed by the mere wealth of the *nouveaux riches*, full of wisdom, the teachers and models of ethics, scientific reasoning, and dignified manners. This may seem a ridiculous fantasy, but after all, as Kroeber has shown, the full flowering of the arts and sciences typically follows a civilization's economic and political decline. Old proper Boston families are well-eclipsed in wealth and power by a great many Texans today but which are considered the more cultured?

In the absence of general war, which is the only basis of calculation we can choose, the future is not necessarily so dismal as the word "fall" would imply. Falling behind some other continent is a relative state and need not imply even a standard of living lower than the present. However this may be, peace is necessary. As things stand now, our policies are ineffectual and much of the presently nonindustrialized world fears, hates, or at best distrusts the West, and particularly the U.S.A. Can anything be salvaged? Could we not face the future at least with some dignity if not equanimity?

The world today can be described from an American's point of view only as one of present disruptions and impending catastrophes. Only a few years ago America's position was secure and the rest of the world, to the extent we perceived it at all, needed no intervention or even advice from us. If one of the troubles with the world was that "there are so many foreigners in it," this irritation could be expected to diminish with the progress and enlightenment which would lead the foreigners to become more like ourselves. But now the world appears to have been made revolutionary by communists. If communists can be successfully combated or at least "contained," then things will right themselves. This seems to be the political wisdom of the day. But obviously something is wrong, for it is more than apparent that we have not contained anything. The point is, the Western nations have failed completely to comprehend the nature of the evolution and spread of industrial civilization.

The "revolution" people worry so much about today is caused by the same industrialization that we know so well as the cause of our own transformation. But if it is the same one then why are the effects so different? Why is it so disruptive? Why does it result in so much aggression, and particularly why does it seem to create dictatorship and tyranny, at least in Russia and China, when it previously caused democracy to flourish in the Western world? Is it not some extra factor such as the teachings of Karl Marx or Lenin (or *somebody!*), or that all dictators are by definition "mad" and out to conquer the world?

It is the same industrial evolution, but there are some profound differences in the modern consequences of it. In some respects exactly opposite effects are created by the *evolution* of an industrial system in the area of its birth as opposed to its *propagation* in a new land. A number of these differences should now be specified.

In Western Europe and North America technological evolution had small beginnings and an organic-like, integrated development. Social, political, and ideological changes, with well-known difficulties, "lagged" but ultimately followed after. Eventually, and particularly clearly in the U.S.A., a total culture in all its various respects became adapted in a sort of moving equilibrium to the progress of industry. But it is important to remember that the beginnings were small—the basic industries were literally backyard affairs—and consequently the amount of capital needed was small enough that it could be provided by private individuals. Then as industry grew so did capital.

Second, the growth of industry was unchallenged by

previously industrialized nations or power-blocs in the rest of the world. Western industry was the *first* industry; its dominance and its independence from the threat of dominance by others was assured. The greatest impediment to the evolutionary potential of the new industry was the problem of readapting the social, political and ideological crust of culture from the feudal-agricultural era, and this crust was finally broken up and transformed.

Evolution, whether biological or cultural, has, as we have seen, a perfectly normal leapfrog effect which makes backward forms potentially more effective than advanced forms in the course of moving into a new stage. But also, an advanced culture or biological species has dominance powers which can obstruct or impede the realization of that potentiality in the backward ones. This causes conflict of a certain kind in recent history; it has caused the spread of a high evolutionary stage to appear in new areas in the form of *revolution*. We see it as a conflict of political ideas, but more is involved than political ideas or ideals. The important thing to recognize is that the characteristics of the evolution of Western industrial civilization are reversed in the areas now industrializing or about to industrialize.

First, the new areas cannot industrialize with small beginnings, as did the West, and then proceed through the original stages of growth, creating capital in the process. They will begin with the latest and most advanced of the known technologies and attempt to create the complete industrial complex at once, skipping whole epochs of our development. This requires a huge capital investment. The economy, therefore, must be socialistic; the government rather than private persons provides most of the capital by necessity. It also means that if capital is not otherwise available to the government it must be extracted from the subsistence-oriented peasantry, as happened first in Russia and is now happening in China. The significance of this situation is that the extraction of capital must be forced. This is the most important *internal* cause of the police state, of despotic government.

The second reversal of the Western industrial experience is that new areas such as Russia and now China (and tomorrow perhaps India, Indonesia, Africa and South America) have been forced to begin their industrialization in the face of challenge and opposition from outside powers. This is the *external* cause of the rise of the police state and of its attitude of belligerence toward the Western world. The dominance of the West was broken by force and the East is not about to back down. We wish to emphasize that tyranny, dictatorships, aggressive military attitudes, and so on, have causes, external and internal, and that by recognizing them we may formulate a policy which could mitigate them and reduce the probability of future violence and war in the continuing industrialization of the One World of the future.

It is uncommon in the U.S.A. to think of modern dictatorships as having causes. Ordinarily, we think of *democracy* as being caused—by our Wise Forefathers, by Education, by the Protestant Ethic, or by Great Writers or Leaders—whereas dictatorships arise spontaneously if the citizenry relaxes its vigilance, or if it is uneducated, or if its national character remains "authoritarian," or if politics remains confounded with "personalism," and so on. But the view of the eminent political scientist Franz Neumann (1950) that a state is as "strong" (as coercive) *as it needs to be*, that it responds to threatening circumstances, is much more useful.

It is interesting that in some contexts the average American does accept this scientific view, however contradictory it is to the usual and more general feeling. McCarthyism was excused by many because they believed that there was danger, a need for greater intervention by the state into the private lives of its citizens. Even more common is the reply given when a foreigner cites the antidemocratic practices of whites with respect to Negroes in the U.S.A. The American describes the historical circumstances in the deep South, or says that the presence of Negroes makes land values fall in the suburbs in the North, and so on. He gives *causes* for this lack of freedom.

The third reversal of the Western industrial evolution is that of the sequential order of culture change. As noted, the West began with a gradual technological development and its "revolution" was the disorder involved in the subsequent adaptive changes in the social, political, and ideological aspects of culture. We expect agreement on this: that the original evolution proceeds from its basic techno-economic aspect, the prime mover, to consequent adaptive changes in the parts of culture progressively further removed from it. However, as Western civilization has spread and influenced more primitive areas, the experience there is frequently the opposite. The ideology comes to them first, often in the absence of any technological change. Thus we speak, nowadays, of the "war for men's minds," as though the future of the world, and particularly of the U.S.A., depended on the outcome of the ideological struggle between East and West.

There are certain characteristics of modern times that have tended to increase the significance of ideas in world affairs. One is, of course, the increased range and intensity of communication between cultural systems. Another is that the partial dominance of the advanced industrial powers over the others has typically fostered in the latter the acceptance of many of the ideas and values of the West, sometimes, as Chapter IV points out, as a defensive or protective measure. The third factor is the grand scale of Western technology. In earlier times, dominant colonial powers directly impeded the spread of advanced technology to their colonies, and to some extent this is still true of the West's policies. In any case, the scale of the technology is now so great, its composition so complex, and the required capital so large that it cannot be readily borrowed except as ideas and plans. Thus we have in many quarters of the globe a new and prevalent ideology and sometimes the political forms receptive to, even demanding, the modern technology that belongs with it. All anthropologists are aware of the great frustration in many nonindustrialized nations that this situation fosters.

This "upside-down effect," or better, "inverse cultural lag," is in our day probably the most widespread kind of change in cultural organization and certainly one of the most important ones for us to understand. Robert Redfield's description of the Mayan peasant village of Chan Kom as the "village that chose progress" is an excellent illustration of a fairly standard process in the world of today: already evolved ideological and political traits of the industrial society have spread to the peasant societies and have had a profound effect. It is a kind of specific adaptation demonstrating a characteristic sequence in piecemeal borrowing from a higher culture. In Ghana we find, for example, a modern political system with its appropriate ideology, but without the industrial foundation. This new society cannot evolve suspended like an air plant and it and the rest of Africa knows this. The struggle by the West to preserve its world dominance is in some very significant respects a war for men's minds, but the final success of the new nations will depend on the support of the ideological and political aspects of the imported culture by the appropriate economic and technological foundations.

Perhaps the most striking of the ideological components of Western civilization that has been accepted, at least in part, by the nonindustrialized nations is that of science, and particularly medical science and practices. Medical science followed the industrial evolution of the West and the increases in productivity kept pace with the expansion of population that medical knowledge caused. But now we witness inverse cultural lag in other areas; medical knowledge is creating a completely unprecedented rise in the favorable birth-death ratio, largely in the areas which already have the greatest pressure of population on resources. At the present rate of increase the earth's population will be doubled by the year 2,000; in only four decades the human race could increase by the amount it has taken one million years of cultural evolution to accomplish! The countries undergoing this transformation need to increase production tremendously. Some, such as China, are apparently determined to do it at all costs, *as they must*. Other areas may be expected to face this reality soon if they have not already.

The industrialization of Russia and the present attempts of China should be recognized as forced-draft processes; they began and continue to industrialize in the face of the West's attempted dominance, and because of lack of capital they are forced to terrorize many of their own people. This internal despotism and the external aggressive (and defensive) military attitudes are the characteristics which most distinguish modern communism from a more ideally conceived, more democratic socialism.

The development of industry in the West, with the mass education and the economic and social mobility which economic progress creates, fostered a new kind of personal freedom and equality. It could elsewhere, too. The democracy that is possible may not involve the freedom for individuals to own giant industries; most of the new areas will be socialistically industrialized in large part, for the basic capital will be manipulated by their governments. But in the absence of opposition from the West and with basic capital lent, given, or otherwise provided, a nontyrannical industrialization is possible.

Communism is neither the cause of what is happening to the world today nor the cause of the West's deteriorating position. The prior industrial evolution of the West is the cause and communism is one of its earliest results. As Barbara Ward, a British political economist specializing in underdeveloped areas, put it (1959: 58):

The Western powers themselves launched every one of the world's contemporary revolutions. They carried them across the oceans and around the world. They set in motion the vast forces of contemporary change and in doing so never doubted that what they did was of profound concern to the entire human race. Yet today, wealthy, complacent, unimaginative, they appear indifferent to the stirring, protean world of change and revolution in which three quarters of the human race is struggling for the forms of a new life. There is not a single Western initiative that embraces change, not one idea or policy for which the sustained Western dedication is forthcoming. In our contemporary world, in short, the idealists of the West appear to think of nothing beyond their material interests, while the materialists of the East seek to remake the face of the earth by the force of their ideas.

It must be apparent by now that we are suggesting a policy that will aid as much and as rapidly as possible, rather than continue to impede, the industrialization of the rest of the world. And we mean *the rest of the world*, not merely small portions of it selected for their political compliance or strategic location. But we have also argued from the law of evolutionary potential that some of the backward areas will probably move beyond us. Is this not a paradox? Would not aiding them in this be something like digging our own grave?

It is not digging our own grave to abolish the causes of strife, despotism, and militarism, but the only way to save ourselves and the world at the same time, for we and the world are in this crisis indivisible. It would be a policy for *us* at the same time it is a policy for the non-industrialized nations. To cease our opposition and our unworkable containment policy would certainly lessen world tensions. Then the next great need is capital for the new industrialization. It must, of course, be capital with "no strings." To abolish tariffs and quotas against the exports of the typical products of nonindustrialized areas—raw materials and metals, unprocessed food, and cheap textiles, for example—is one obvious way to begin. International monetary funds, but on a scale not even visualized today, should be next. If we *share*, in the interests of the whole human race, we win; that is, democracy and humanity win as the internal and external causes of conflict and tyranny are abolished. If we do not, we are trifling stupidly and unconscionably with our chances for survival.

All this follows from the logical application of the laws of evolutionary potential and of dominance to the history and present situation of the world. It is probably sensible to add, however, that we should realistically recognize the character of our government and public opinion today. In all probability the U.S.A. will not initiate the recommended policy on the necessary scale, at least in the near future. The world will probably continue to be in terrible danger for some years to come.

Perhaps the best justification for this long discussion of the modern world is that it is another example of the explanatory and predictive uses of the evolutionary laws. We take it as our responsibility to formulate some ideas and opinions about modern times that can be argued on scientific grounds, just as we strive to interpret such things as the evolution of writing, the origins of agriculture, or the rise and fall of the ancient civilizations in the Mediterranean. It is the first job of science to try to understand things, today's things as well as remote things. Yet it is also our job to make our opinions known. How can we, as scientists, believe other than that man's ills are due as much to his ignorance as to his nature?

E. B. Tylor said it in 1881: ". . . the study of man and civilization is not only a matter of scientific interest, but at once passes into the practical business of life. We have in it the means of understanding our own lives and our place in the world, vaguely and imperfectly it is true, but at any rate more clearly than any former generation. The knowledge of man's course of life, from the remote past to the present, will not only help us to forecast the future, but may guide us in our duty of leaving the world better than we found it."

Of course Tylor wrote in braver days than ours, but might we not at least work in the hope that when we leave the world it will still be intact?

Note

This book is another instance of that common phenomenon in scholarship, the chapter that got out of control. The subjects treated here in separate chapters were originally parts of a single chapter of a general work on which we (Sahlins and Service) had begun to collaborate in 1958. By the next spring that chapter had acquired a life of its own and now it appears here, expanded and revised, while the parent book remains still far from finished.

The ideas as first set down seemed so fundamental to us and the treatment so often novel that we decided to give them a professional hearing. We therefore arranged to present a symposium, "Principles of Culture Evolution," at the 1959 annual meeting of the Central States Branch of the American Anthropological Association (Madison, Wisconsin, May 14–16). We then asked two friends, graduate students at the University of Michigan, to participate in the writing and delivery of the papers. Much of the specific elaboration of the ideas in Chapters III and IV, therefore, was the work of Thomas Harding and David Kaplan, and we are very grateful to them. Thus, after the Introduction, of which we are the joint authors, Chapter II is by Marshall D. Sahlins, Chapter III by Thomas G. Harding, Chapter IV by David Kaplan, and Chapter V by Elman R. Service.

We must acknowledge a great deal of intellectual aid. Our scholarly dependence has been largely on the classical evolutionists, Herbert Spencer, Lewis H. Morgan, and E. B.

Tylor. This book is not a "parrot's cry," however. A good deal of what is basic here is implicit if not explicit in the work of those men, it is true, but they did not elaborate or explain their theory very much. Apparently in their day there was no need for argumentation, but since then there has been much misunderstanding of the evolutionist position and there are also some new problems. There is a need for an explication addressed to the modern audience.

Our foremost indebtedness among the contemporary scientists is to Leslie A. White because, in addition to the use of his writings, we were fortunate enough to have been his students. Without this experience we would not have had the interest or training to appreciate the earlier evolutionists. Just how we are to describe accurately his contribution to the particular ideas of this book, however, we do not know. Perhaps it is simplest to say that there is a generic continuity from him to us (as from teacher to students) but some specific discontinuity (caused by the varying independent concerns of grownups). Some of the generalizations about evolution that we have formulated here came as a surprise to us and perhaps they will to him.

Several colleagues have read the manuscript and offered useful suggestions. We are particularly indebted to Morton H. Fried, who was the formal discussant at the Madison symposium. Our subsequent reworking of the chapters owes a great deal to his intelligent and painstaking critique. We also acknowledge with gratitude the aid of Robert M. Adams, Robert Carneiro, Marshall T. Newman, Barbara Sahlins, Helen Service, James Spuhler, and Eric Wolf.

Sahlins would like to acknowledge a Faculty Research Fellowship granted him by the Social Science Research Council. The distinction between specific and general evolution that is developed in Chapter II originated as a by-product of research underwritten by the award.

Ann Arbor   Marshall D. Sahlins
                             Elman R. Service

Bibliography

Barnett, H. G. 1938 The nature of the potlatch. American Anthropologist 40: 349–58.

Barth, Fredrik 1956 Ecologic relationship of ethnic groups in Swat, North Pakistan. American Anthropologist 58: 1079–89.

Beardsley, Richard K. 1953 Hypotheses on inner Asian pastoral nomadism and its culture area. In Asia and North America: Transpacific Contacts, pp. 24–28. Memoirs of the Society of American Archaeology No. 9.

Bettelheim, Charles 1959 China's economic growth. Monthly Review 10: 429–58.

Birdsell, Joseph B. 1957 On methods of evolutionary biology and anthropology: Part II, Anthropology. American Scientist 45: 393–400.

Blum, Harold F. 1955 Time's arrow and evolution. Princeton, Princeton University Press.

Boas, Franz 1928 Anthropology and modern life. New York, Norton.

Boyd, William C. 1950 Genetics and the races of man. Boston, Heath.

Braidwood, Robert J. 1948 Prehistoric men. Chicago, Chicago Natural History Museum Press.

Braidwood, Robert J. and Charles A. Reed 1957 The achievement and early consequences of food production: a consideration of the archaeological and natural historical evidence. *In* Cold Spring Harbor Symposia on Quantitative Biology 22: 19–31.

Chi, Ch'ao-Ting   1934   The economic basis of unity and division in Chinese history. Pacific Affairs 7: 386–94.

Childe, V. Gordon   1946   What happened in history. New York, Penguin.

   1951   Social evolution. New York, Schuman.

   1958   The prehistory of European society. London, Penguin.

Clough, Shepard B.   1951   The rise and fall of civilization. New York, McGraw-Hill.

Codere, Helen   1950   Fighting with property, a study of Kwakiutl potlatching and warfare, 1792–1930. Monographs of the American Ethnological Society, 18. New York.

Cole, G. D. H.   1934   What Marx really meant. London, Gollancz.

Colson, Elizabeth   1953   The Makah Indians. Manchester, Manchester University Press.

Cook, Sherburne F.   1943   The conflict between the California Indian and white civilization: the Indian versus the Spanish Mission. Ibero-Americana 21. Berkeley, University of California Press.

Cottrell, Fred   1955   Energy and society. New York, McGraw-Hill.

Drucker, Philip   1951   The northern and central Nootkan tribes. Bureau of American Ethnology Bulletin 144, Washington, D.C.

   1955   Indians of the northwest coast. New York, McGraw-Hill.

Forde, C. Daryll   1957   Habitat, economy and society. London, Methuen.

Fried, Morton H.   1952   Land tenure, geography and ecology in the contact of cultures. The American Journal of Economics and Sociology 11: 391–412.

   1957   The classification of corporate unilineal descent

groups. The Journal of the Royal Anthropological Society 87: 1–129.

Gillin, John P. 1948 The ways of man. New York, Appleton-Century-Crofts.

Greenberg, Joseph 1957 Essays in linguistics. Viking Fund Publications in Anthropology 24. New York.
1959 Language and evolution. *In* Evolution and Anthropology: A Centennial Appraisal, pp. 61–75. The Anthropological Society of Washington, Washington, D.C.

Haag, William G. 1959 The status of evolutionary theory in American archaeology. *In* Evolution and Anthropology: A Centennial Appraisal, pp. 90–105. The Anthropological Society of Washington, Washington, D.C.

Harding, Thomas G. Some techniques of communication in four aboriginal American cultures. Ms.

Harris, Marvin 1959 The economy has no surplus? American Anthropologist 61: 185–99.

Hatt, Gudmund 1953 Plough and pasture: Part II, Farming of non-European peoples. New York, Schuman.

Herskovits, Melville J. 1941 Economics and anthropology: a rejoinder. Journal of Political Economy 49: 273.
1945 The processes of cultural change. *In* The Science of Man in the World Crisis, Ralph Linton, ed., pp. 143–70. New York, Columbia University Press.
1948 Man and his works. New York, Knopf.

Hughes, H. Stuart 1949 An essay for our times. New York, Knopf.

Huxley, Julian S. 1943 Evolution: the modern synthesis. New York and London, Harper.
1956 Evolution, cultural and biological. *In* Current Anthropology, W. L. Thomas Jr., ed., pp. 3–25. Chicago, University of Chicago Press.

James, William 1880 Great men, great thoughts, and the environment. Atlantic Monthly 46: 441–59.

Jochelson, Waldemar   1905–8   Material culture and social organization of the Koryak. American Museum of Natural History Memoir 10, Part 2.

1933   The Yakut. American Museum of Natural History, Anthropological Papers 33: 37–225.

Keller, Albert G.   1947   Societal evolution. New Haven, Yale University Press.

Kirk, G. S. and J. E. Raven   1957   The presocratic philosophers. Cambridge, Cambridge University Press.

Kluckhohn, Clyde   1959   The role of evolutionary thought in anthropology. *In* Evolution and Anthropology: A Centennial Appraisal, pp. 144–57. The Anthropological Society of Washington, Washington, D.C.

Kroeber, Alfred L.   1939   Cultural and natural areas of native North America. Berkeley, University of California Press.

1943   Franz Boas: the man. *In* Franz Boas: 1858–1942, A. L. Kroeber et al., p. 5. American Anthropological Association Memoir 61.

1946   History and evolution. Southwestern Journal of Anthropology 2: 14.

1952   The nature of culture. Chicago, University of Chicago Press.

Lattimore, Owen   1938   The geographical factor in Mongol history. Geographical Journal 91: 11–16.

1940   Inner Asia frontiers of China. American Geographical Society Research Series No. 21.   New York.

1947   Inner Asian frontiers: Chinese and Russian margins of expansion. Journal of Economic History 7: 24–52.

Laufer, Berthold   1918   Review of R. H. Lowie, Culture and ethnology. American Anthropologist 20: 90.

Linton, Ralph   1936   The study of man. New York, Appleton-Century.

1955   The tree of culture. New York, Knopf.

Lotka, Alfred J.   1922   Contribution to the energetics of

evolution. Proceedings of the National Academy of Science 8: 147–51.

1945 The law of evolution as a maximal principle. Human Biology 17: 167–94.

Lowie, Robert H. 1940 An introduction to cultural anthropology. New York, Farrar and Rinehart.

Mead, Margaret 1958 Cultural determinants of behavior. *In* Behavior and Evolution, Anne Rowe and G. G. Simpson, eds., pp. 480–503. New Haven, Yale University Press.

Mills, C. Wright 1959 The sociological imagination. New York, Oxford University Press.

Murdock, George Peter 1949 Social structure. New York, MacMillan.

1959 Evolution in social organization. *In* Evolution and Anthropology: A Centennial Appraisal, pp. 126–43. The Anthropological Society of Washington, Washington, D.C.

Neumann, Franz L. 1950 Approaches to the study of political power. Political Science Quarterly 65: 161–80.

Pearson, Oliver P. 1948 Metabolism and bioenergetics. Scientific Monthly 66: 131–34.

Roosevelt, Theodore 1910 Biological analogies in history. New York, Oxford University Press.

Russell, Bertrand 1927 Outline of Philosophy. London, Allen and Unwin.

Sahlins, Marshall D. 1955 Esoteric efflorescence in Easter Island. American Anthropologist 57: 1045–52.

1958 Social stratification in Polynesia. Seattle, University of Washington Press.

Secoy, Frank Raymond 1953 Changing military patterns on the Great Plains. Monographs of the American Ethnological Society 21. New York.

Simpson, George Gaylord 1950 The meaning of evolution. New Haven, Yale University Press.

1958 The study of evolution: methods and present status of theory. *In* Behavior and Evolution, Anne Roe and G. G. Simpson, eds., pp. 7–26. New Haven, Yale University Press.

Spencer, Herbert 1897 The principles of sociology. Vol. 3. New York, D. Appleton and Company.

Sternberg, Fritz 1951 Capitalism and socialism on trial. Translated from the German by Edward Fitzgerald. New York, John Day.

Steward, Julian H. 1949 Cultural causality and law: a trial formulation of the development of early civilizations. American Anthropologist 51: 1–27.

1953 Evolution and process. *In* Anthropology Today, A. L. Kroeber, ed., pp. 313–26. Chicago, University of Chicago Press.

1955 Theory of culture change: the methodology of multilinear evolution. Urbana, University of Illinois Press.

1956 Cultural evolution. The Scientific American 194, No. 5: 75.

Tocqueville, Alexis de 1954 Democracy in America. 2 vols. New York, Vintage ed.

Trotsky, Leon n.d. The history of the Russian revolution. Ann Arbor, University of Michigan Press.

Turney-High, Harry 1949 General anthropology. New York, Crowell.

Tylor, Edward B. 1871 Primitive culture. 2 vols. London, Murray.

1904 Anthropology: an introduction to the study of man and civilization. New York, Appleton.

Veblen, Thorstein 1915 Imperial Germany and the industrial revolution. New York, MacMillan.

Ward, Barbara 1959 A new economic strategy. The Atlantic 203, No. 2: 56–60.

Wedel, Waldo R. 1941 Environment and native subsistence economies in the central Great Plains. Smithsonian Miscellaneous Collections 101, No. 3. Washington, D.C.

Wells, H. G., Julian S. Huxley and G. R. Wells 1934 The science of life. New York, Literary Guild.

Bibliography

White, Leslie A. 1945 History, evolutionism, and functionalism: three types of interpretation of culture. Southwestern Journal of Anthropology 1: 221–48.

1949 The science of culture. New York, Farrar Straus. Paperbound ed. 1958, Grove Press.

1959 The evolution of culture. New York, McGraw-Hill.

1959a The concept of evolution in cultural anthropology: *In* Evolution and Anthropology: A Centennial Appraisal, pp. 106–25. The Anthropological Society of Washington, Washington, D.C.

Wolf, Eric 1957 Closed corporate peasant communities in Mesoamerica and Central Java. Southwestern Journal of Anthropology 13: 1–18.

Zimmermann, Erich W. 1951 World resources and industries. New York, Harper.

Ann Arbor Paperbacks

Waddell, *The Desert Fathers*
Erasmus, *The Praise of Folly*
Donne, *Devotions*
Malthus, *Population: The First Essay*
Berdyaev, *The Origin of Russian Communism*
Einhard, *The Life of Charlemagne*
Edwards, *The Nature of True Virtue*
Gilson, *Héloïse and Abélard*
Aristotle, *Metaphysics*
Kant, *Education*
Boulding, *The Image*
Duckett, *The Gateway to the Middle Ages* (3 vols.): *Italy; France and Britain; Monasticism*
Bowditch and Ramsland, *Voices of the Industrial Revolution*
Luxemburg, *The Russian Revolution* and *Leninism or Marxism?*
Rexroth, *Poems from the Greek Anthology*
Zoshchenko, *Scenes from the Bathhouse*
Thrupp, *The Merchant Class of Medieval London*
Procopius, *Secret History*
Fine, *Laissez Faire and the General-Welfare State*
Adcock, *Roman Political Ideas and Practice*
Swanson, *The Birth of the Gods*
Xenophon, *The March Up Country*
Trotsky, *The New Course*
Buchanan and Tullock, *The Calculus of Consent*
Hobson, *Imperialism*
Pobedonostsev, *Reflections of a Russian Statesman*
Kinietz, *The Indians of the Western Great Lakes 1615–1760*
Bromage, *Writing for Business*
Lurie, *Mountain Wolf Woman, Sister of Crashing Thunder*
Leonard, *Baroque Times in Old Mexico*
Meier, *Negro Thought in America, 1880–1915*
Burke, *The Philosophy of Edmund Burke*
Michelet, *Joan of Arc*
Conze, *Buddhist Thought in India*
Arberry, *Aspects of Islamic Civilization*
Chesnutt, *The Wife of His Youth and Other Stories*
Gross, *Sound and Form in Modern Poetry*
Zola, *The Masterpiece*
Chesnutt, *The Marrow of Tradition*
Aristophanes, *Four Comedies*

Aristophanes, *Three Comedies*
Chesnutt, *The Conjure Woman*
Duckett, *Carolingian Portraits*
Rapoport and Chammah, *Prisoner's Dilemma*
Aristotle, *Poetics*
Boulding, *Beyond Economics*
Peattie, *The View from the Barrio*
Duckett, *Death and Life in the Tenth Century*
Langford, *Galileo, Science and the Church*
McNaughton, *The Taoist Vision*
Anderson, *Matthew Arnold and the Classical Tradition*
Milio, *9226 Kercheval*
Weisheipl, *The Development of Physical Theory in the Middle Ages*
Breton, *Manifestoes of Surrealism*
Gershman, *The Surrealist Revolution in France*
Burt, *Mammals of the Great Lakes Region*
Lester, *Theravada Buddhism in Southeast Asia*
Scholz, *Carolingian Chronicles*
Marković, *From Affluence to Praxis*
Wik, *Henry Ford and Grass-roots America*
Sahlins and Service, *Evolution and Culture*
Wickham, *Early Medieval Italy*
Waddell, *The Wandering Scholars*
Rosenberg, *Bolshevik Visions* (2 parts in 2 vols.)
Mannoni, *Prospero and Caliban*
Aron, *Democracy and Totalitarianism*
Shy, *A People Numerous and Armed*
Taylor, *Roman Voting Assemblies*
Goodfield, *An Imagined World*
Hesiod, *The Works and Days; Theogony; The Shield of Herakles*
Raverat, *Period Piece*
Lamming, *In the Castle of My Skin*
Fisher, *The Conjure-Man Dies*
Strayer, *The Albigensian Crusades*
Lamming, *The Pleasures of Exile*
Lamming, *Natives of My Person*
Glaspell, *Lifted Masks and Other Works*
Wolff, *Aesthetics and the Sociology of Art*
Grand, *The Heavenly Twins*
Cornford, *The Origin of Attic Comedy*
Allen, *Wolves of Minong*
Brathwaite, *Roots*
Fisher, *The Walls of Jericho*
Lamming, *The Emigrants*